Grammar and Writing 7

Student Workbook

First Edition

Christie Curtis

Mary Hake

Houghton Mifflin Harcourt Publishers, Inc.

Grammar and Writing 7

First Edition

Student Workbook

ISBN-13: 978-1-4190-9855-0
ISBN-10:   1-4190-9855-1

Houghton Mifflin Harcourt Publishers, Inc.
181 Ballardvale Street
Wilmington, MA 01887

http://saxonhomeschool.com

Printed in the United States of America.

1 2 3 4 5 6 7 8 862 16 15 14 13 12 11 10 09

Student Workbook 7 Contents

Writing Lessons

www.saxonhomeschool.com
©Houghton Mifflin Harcourt Publishers, Inc.

Grammar and Writing 7
Student Workbook, 9781419098550

More Practice and Slapstick Stories

Introduction

The ability to communicate clearly and effectively in writing connects us with people and enhances our prospects for future success in school and in the workplace. We improve our writing skills with practice. Daily journals and informal letters, notes, or emails to friends and family members provide frequent opportunities to use what we have learned in our grammar and writing lessons. In addition, we must practice more formal writing exercises to prepare ourselves for writing assignments that we will receive in high school and college classes.

In *Grammar and Writing 6*, we learned to create topic sentences and to develop body paragraphs, introductory paragraphs, and concluding paragraphs in order to write different kinds of five-paragraph essays. We also wrote summaries and research papers. In *Grammar and Writing 7*, we shall write additional expository, persuasive, descriptive, and narrative essays. Then we shall expand our writing experience to include imaginative stories, more chapter and short story summaries, longer research papers, and even some poetry.

Keeping your daily journals and your writing assignments in a folder or binder will help you to organize your work so that you can easily refer back to earlier assignments when necessary.

Writing
Lessons

Review Lesson: The Paragraph

The Paragraph A **paragraph** is a group of sentences that builds on a main idea, or topic. A good paragraph presents one main idea and develops it with additional sentences giving more specific information about that main idea. The supporting sentences are arranged in a logical order.

The Topic Sentence The **topic sentence** is a complete sentence telling the main idea of a paragraph. Often the topic sentence is the first sentence of a paragraph, but not always. Topic sentences are underlined in the following paragraphs:

> Jasper loves the sea. Every summer he camps out on the beach where he can hear the sound of the crashing waves night and day. Walking for miles along the shore, fishing from the pier, and swimming in the surf are his favorite activities.

> As Karina was brushing her teeth this morning, she noticed a small battalion of ants marching around the faucet. At lunch time she found several ants crawling around in the plastic bread bag. And by evening, an entire army of ants had found its way into her kitchen cupboards and were feasting on peanut butter, jelly, crackers, and cereal. Karina faced a major ant invasion today.

Example 1 Arrange all of the sentences below in a logical order to create one good paragraph. Then underline the topic sentence.

5 • Finally, towel dry any excess drops of water from the clean window.

4 • Then use the squeegee to wipe the soapy water from the window.

1 • To wash a window, you will need a bucket of soapy water, a scrubber, a rubber squeegee, and a towel.

2 • Once you have gathered your materials, you are ready to begin washing.

3 • First use the scrubber to wet the window and remove dirt and grease.

We sequence the sentences to make this paragraph:

> To wash a window, you will need a bucket of soapy water, a scrubber, a rubber squeegee, and a towel. Once you have gathered your materials, you are ready to begin washing. First use the scrubber to wet the window and remove dirt and grease. Then use the squeegee to wipe the soapy water from the window. Finally, towel dry any excess drops of water from the clean window.

Example 2 Underline the topic sentence in the following paragraph:

>Every time Ms. Wright gives her English class a writing assignment, Dudley groans. Dudley hates writing. He says he can't spell or even think of anything to write. Writing makes his brain hurt, his palms sweat, and his eyes twitch.

We see that the paragraph above is all about how Dudley hates writing. Therefore, we underline the topic sentence as follows:

>Every time Ms. Wright gives her English class a writing assignment, Dudley groans. **<u>Dudley hates writing</u>**. He says he can't spell or even think of anything to write. Writing makes his brain hurt, his palms sweat, and his eyes twitch.

Practice Arrange the sentences below in a logical order to create a good paragraph. Write the paragraph on the lines provided. Then underline the topic sentence.

Answers for this Practice are found on the last page of the Writing packet.

4 • Just as she was ready to give up the search, Misty found Scamp sleeping peacefully behind the sofa in the living room.

3 • Then she searched through the garage, the backyard, and the front yard.

1 • When Misty came home from school, she discovered that her cat, Scamp, was missing.

2 • First she walked up and down the street, calling his name.

_____

_____

_____

_____

_____

_____

_____

_____

_____

_____

Underline the topic sentence in each paragraph below.

During math and social studies, Dudley draws cute little elves in his notebook with a pencil. Sometimes science lectures inspire him to draw exotic plants and animals. His notebook is full of intricate and interesting sketches. Dudley is an outstanding doodler!

I've never seen a bird as peculiar as the heron. A wading bird found in temperate and tropical regions, the heron has long thin legs with knobby knees. Its neck is so long and slender that I wonder how it can swallow anything. Its pointed bill and unusual head feathers give the heron an appearance unlike any other bird I've seen.

Lillian has read hundreds of stories about the wild West, and she can recite them all word for word. Lillian dreams of becoming a cowgirl someday. You'll never see her wearing anything but Western attire—jeans with chaps, boots, and a bandana. Although she doesn't own a horse, she is saving her money to buy one.

Additional Practice Practice writing a paragraph for at least one of the following topic sentences.

1. We should choose our friends carefully.

2. Summer is an enjoyable time of the year.

3. Writing a good paragraph is an important skill.

In the next four lessons, we shall practice writing and evaluating five-paragraph essays.

Parts of a Complete Essay

Our goal is to write clear, coherent, focused essays. To accomplish this, we must keep in mind the structure of a complete essay. In this lesson, we shall briefly review the **parts of a complete essay.**

Complete Essay

A **complete essay** is constructed of three main parts:

1. Introductory Paragraph

2. Body or Support Paragraphs

3. Concluding Paragraph

Now let us recall all that is included in these three main parts of an essay.

Introductory Paragraph

The **introductory paragraph,** the first paragraph of an essay, introduces the general theme or subject of the essay. To do this, and to attract the reader's interest, the introductory paragraph contains a very clear sentence that tells exactly what the entire essay will be about. That one, very clear sentence comes near the beginning of the introductory paragraph and is called the *thesis statement.* For this reason, the introductory paragraph is often called the *thesis paragraph.*

Thesis Statement

Every essay that attempts to persuade, influence, or explain something must have a **thesis statement** in the introductory paragraph. The thesis statement not only tells the reader exactly what the essay is about but also clearly states the writer's position on the topic.

Introductory Sentence

The first sentence of an essay, the **introductory sentence,** should grab the reader's interest. This sentence can be long or short. It can be opinion or fact. It can even be more than one sentence. It is an introduction to the thesis statement, and it should make the reader want to know more about the subject of the essay.

Body Paragraphs	**Body paragraphs,** or support paragraphs, come after the first paragraph and before the final paragraph. Body paragraphs prove your point, and they provide the information that makes the reader understand exactly what you, the writer, want to communicate.
Topic Sentence	A **topic sentence** is a complete sentence, usually at the beginning of a body paragraph. It tells the reader exactly what the paragraph is about and is followed by supporting sentences.
Supporting Sentences: Experiences	**Experience sentences,** relating stories or events that you have experienced or observed, may follow a topic sentence to begin to create a full body paragraph.
Supporting Sentences: Opinions	Your opinions are your thoughts or feelings about a particular subject. **Opinion sentences,** communicating thoughts and feelings that are directly related to the topic sentence, may follow experience sentences to further develop the body paragraph.
Supporting Sentences: Facts, Examples, or Other Kinds	Some kinds of essays require more than just experience and opinion to prove a point. **Facts** or **examples** from research are sometimes necessary to support a thesis or the topic sentence of a body paragraph. Other kinds of sentences, which we shall discuss in a later lesson, include definitions, anecdotes, arguments, and analogies.
Transition	A **transition** is a word, phrase, or clause that links one subject or idea to another. A transition is placed at the beginning of a body paragraph to help the essay "flow" from one paragraph to another. Effective transitions make the ideas easier for the reader to follow. Typical transitions include the following:

Another thing…	Likewise…
The second reason…	Similarly…
Furthermore…	In the same way…
As a result…	Consequently…
However…	On the other hand…
Therefore…	In conclusion…

Concluding Paragraph The final paragraph of an essay, the **concluding paragraph**, should both summarize and reinforce the ideas and opinions expressed in the body of the essay. The concluding paragraph includes two important parts:

1. a restatement of the thesis statement
2. a reference to each of the topic sentences

Good writers know that "last words" leave a lasting impression.

Example Here is an example of a five-paragraph essay that contains all the essential parts:

introductory sentence

Introductory Paragraph

Why should we learn to write well? *The ability to communicate clearly and effectively in writing connects us with people and enhances our prospects for future success in school and in the workplace.*

thesis statement (italics)

Body Paragraphs

In the first place, writing well allows us to communicate with other people. We can share our thoughts and feelings with others by writing personal letters, business letters, notes, and emails. Often, people's friendships and/or business relationships are dependent on their ability to keep in touch with people by way of written correspondence.

Secondly, our success in school both now and in the future depends on our ability to write well. Teachers may require us to be able to express on paper what we have learned in classes such as social studies, English, and science. We will also need to be able to write effectively on college applications.

In addition, we shall use our writing skills in our future work place. A well-written job application might help us to acquire the job we desire. Moreover, most jobs and professions entail writing. Teachers, doctors, pastors, secretaries, mechanics, and business people all have to write daily in their workplaces.

Concluding Paragraph

In conclusion, the ability to write skillfully will help us in our relationships with people, in our schooling, and in our future workplace. No skill is more important to our success than writing.

restatement of thesis with reference to each topic sentence

In the essay above, transitions are circled and topic sentences are underlined.

Refer to the sample five-paragraph essay from the previous page to complete 1–5 on the blank lines provided.

1. Write the thesis statement of the essay.

   _____

2. Write the introductory sentence of the essay.

   _____

3. Write the topic sentence for the first body paragraph.

   _____

4. Write the word group used as a transition for the first body paragraph of the essay. _____

5. Write the words used as a transition to the concluding paragraph. _____

A Memory Tool

The chart below helps us remember the essential parts of a complete, five-paragraph essay.

ESSAY PLAN	
Introductory Paragraph	Introductory Sentence(s) Thesis Statement
Body or Support Paragraph	*Topic Sentence* Support Sentences: Experience, Opinion, Fact, Example, or Other
Body or Support Paragraph	*Topic Sentence* Support Sentences: Experience, Opinion, Fact, Example, or Other
Body or Support Paragraph	*Topic Sentence* Support Sentences: Experience, Opinion, Fact, Example, or Other
Concluding Paragraph	Restatement of the thesis Reference to each topic sentence

Example   Study the chart from the previous page. Then try to reproduce it from memory on a separate piece of paper.

We simply use this chart as a memory tool to help us keep in mind the structure of a complete essay. We may abbreviate in order to reproduce it quickly.

Essay Plan	
Intro. Para.	Intro. Sent. Thesis Statement
Body Para.	Top. Sent. Sup. Sents.: Exp., Op., Fact, Ex., or Other
B. P.	T. S. S. S.: Exp., Op., Fact, Ex., or Other
B. P.	T. S. S. S.: Exp., Op., Fact, Ex., or Other
Concl. Para.	Restatement of thesis Ref. to each T. S.

Practice   Study the chart showing the parts of a five-paragraph essay. Then reproduce it from memory, abbreviating if you wish. After checking your reproduction of the chart to be sure it contains all the essential parts, place this assignment in your folder or binder for quick reference in the future.

LESSON 2

Preparing to Write a Complete Essay

The Thesis Statement

Keeping in mind the structure of a complete essay described in Lesson 1, we will prepare to write a five-paragraph essay with the following thesis statement:

Fireworks can be dangerous.

Brainstorming

Brainstorming is a method of quickly capturing ideas about a topic or problem. One way to brainstorm is illustrated below.

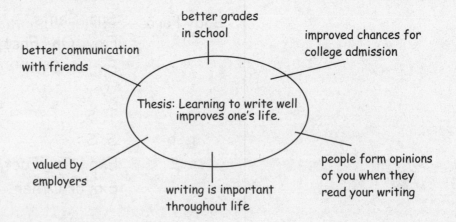

For the next few minutes, use this model to record brainstorming ideas for the thesis statement "Fireworks can be dangerous." In the middle of a blank sheet of paper, draw a circle, three or four inches in diameter. Inside that circle, write the thesis statement. Then quickly begin to write in the area outside the circle any and all words that come into your mind as soon as they come into your mind.

- Write quickly. Do not allow your pencil to stop moving.

- Do not worry about spelling or neatness.

- Do not worry about the word order or location.

- Don't think, just write.

Write for about three minutes or until your paper is covered with words, whichever comes first.

When you have finished, you will almost certainly have several ideas to help you get started writing your essay.

Organizing your Ideas

After you have brainstormed, the next step is to look at the ideas you have generated and identify the ones that best support your thesis statement. Follow these steps to organize your ideas:

1. Take a moment to look at the words or groups of words you wrote. Some of them will begin to stand out as relating very well to the thesis, and others will begin to look as though they don't belong or are not as strong.

2. Choose at least three different words or groups of words that best support the thesis. Circle them. If you cannot decide on just three, you may circle four or five. If you circle more than three words or groups of words, you have more than enough support for your thesis statement. You can write several body paragraphs of support, or you might later decide to combine one or more arguments or to eliminate the weaker ones.

3. These circled word groups will become your body paragraph ideas. Write these ideas on a separate piece of paper leaving space underneath each idea to add more notes later for expanding the paragraphs.

4. Look at your body paragraph ideas and try to determine the order in which they should be arranged in the body of your essay to best support your thesis. Number the ideas. You can rearrange the order or even eliminate or add additional body paragraphs at any time as ideas come to you.

Forming Topic Sentences

Once you have selected the best ideas from your brainstorming and placed them on a separate page, the next step is to take those ideas and form them into topic sentences. Each topic sentence will become a main idea for your essay's body paragraphs.

Practice

Write at least three topic sentences that clearly support your thesis statement. Keep this assignment in your folder or binder. In Lesson 3, we shall expand these topic sentences into body paragraphs and then complete an essay.

LESSON 3

Writing a Complete Essay

In Lesson 2, you brainstormed and created ideas to support the thesis statement "Fireworks can be dangerous." You also chose the best of those ideas and put them in the order that best supports the thesis statement. Then you used the ideas to create topic sentences. Now you are ready to write the complete essay.

Practice Using the topic sentences you wrote for Lesson 2, follow the steps below to complete the essay.

1. For each topic sentence, write a body paragraph to support the thesis statement. To expand your paragraph, you might add experience sentences, opinion sentences, example sentences, and/or fact sentences.

2. Create an introductory paragraph with an introductory sentence that will grab the reader's interest, and a sentence that states the thesis.

3. Write a concluding paragraph that includes a restatement of the thesis and a reference to each of the topic sentences.

4. Add transitions between body paragraphs to make your ideas easier for the reader to follow. Pay special attention to the transition into the concluding paragraph.

5. Finally, put all the parts together to form a complete essay. As you are working, make any necessary corrections to your previous work. You might add or subtract words, or make any other change that results in a more effective essay. Keep this essay in your folder or binder. You will evaluate it in the next lesson.

The Writing Process All of the writing we do should be viewed as "work in progress." Even after you have turned in an essay to your teacher for a grade, you should not feel it can never be touched again. The knowledge that *writing is a process* should guide your thinking throughout the construction of an essay. From the first steps in organizing your thoughts, to creating body paragraphs, to adding transitions, you should feel free to make changes to improve your work.

At each step of the writing process, you should stop to reevaluate both your thoughts and the words you have placed on the page.

It is helpful to do this after each step of the writing process. It is also important to do this after the entire essay is written. In fact, it is probably most helpful to complete an essay, then walk away from it for a day or two, and then come back and read it again.

Many times, sentences that seemed good the first time appear much different a day or two later. Furthermore, you may find that more ideas have come to you, or ideas that were somewhat muddled before have become clearer. Two days later, you can write them in a way that is more meaningful to the reader.

Use the following guidelines to help you evaluate your writing.

Evaluating Your Writing Do not be afraid to change what you have already written. Just because it was typed or written on paper in ink does not mean it cannot be improved.

Ask yourself these questions throughout the writing process:

- Is my introductory sentence interesting? *If it is not interesting to you, it certainly will not be interesting to the reader.*

- Do I have a thesis statement that clearly explains the subject of this essay? (For this assignment, the thesis was given to you.)

- Does my thesis statement clearly state my position?

- Does each body paragraph have a clear topic sentence at the beginning that tells the reader exactly what the paragraph will be about? *Read each topic sentence without the rest of the paragraph to see if it can stand alone as a strong idea.*

- Are there other personal experiences or factual examples that I can add to help improve my credibility and help the reader to better understand my point?

- In my opinion sentences, have I described my emotions and feelings so well that they create a picture in the mind of the reader to help him or her feel the same as I feel?

- Does each paragraph (except for the first) begin with an effective transition?

- Are there other arguments that I can add as additional body paragraphs to help me prove my point?

- Are some of my arguments weak and unconvincing? Should they be removed because they do not help me prove my point?

- Do my body paragraphs appear in the best possible order to prove my point? Could I place them in a different order that is more logical or effective?

- Is each sentence constructed as well as it should be? *Read each sentence in each paragraph as if it were the only sentence on the page. This helps you to catch sentence fragments, run-on sentences, misspellings, and grammatical errors.*

- Does my concluding paragraph summarize and reinforce the ideas and opinions expressed in the essay?

Practice Use the Evaluation Form on the page following this lesson to evaluate the essay you wrote for Lesson 3. Read your essay carefully as you check for the items listed on the Evaluation Form. Write YES or NO in the blank next to each question.

When you are finished, you will either be confident that you have a strong essay, or you will know where it needs to be improved.

If you answered NO to one or more of the questions on the Evaluation Form, rewrite to improve those areas.

When you can answer YES to every question on the Evaluation Form, you will have completed this assignment.

Essay Evaluation Form

Thesis: _____

_____ Is my introductory sentence interesting? *If it is not interesting to you, it certainly won't be interesting to the reader.*

_____ Do I have a thesis statement that clearly explains the subject of this essay?

_____ Does my thesis statement clearly state my position?

_____ Does each body paragraph have a clear topic sentence at the beginning that tells the reader exactly what the paragraph will be about? *Read each topic sentence without the rest of the paragraph to see if it can stand alone as a strong idea.*

_____ Have I included personal experiences that improve my credibility and help the reader to better understand my point?

_____ In my opinion sentences, have I described my emotions and feelings so well that they create a picture in the mind of the reader to help him or her feel the same as I feel?

_____ Does each paragraph (except for the first paragraph) begin with an effective transition?

_____ Are there no other arguments that I can add as additional body paragraphs to help me prove my point?

_____ Are all of my arguments strong and convincing? Do they all help to prove my point?

_____ Do my body paragraphs appear in the best possible order to prove my point? Is their order logical and effective?

_____ Is each sentence structured as well as it could be? *Read each sentence in each paragraph as if it were the only sentence on the page. This helps you catch fragments and run-on sentences and evaluate the overall strength or weakness of each sentence.*

_____ Does my concluding paragraph summarize and reinforce the ideas and opinions expressed in the essay?

www.saxonhomeschool.com
©Houghton Mifflin Harcourt Publishers, Inc.

Grammar and Writing 7
Student Workbook, 9781419098550

Different Ways of Expanding a Topic Sentence into a Paragraph

We have learned that a topic sentence states the main idea of a paragraph and that the remainder of the paragraph should clearly and completely prove that the topic sentence is true.

We have practiced developing a body paragraph by adding experience and opinion sentences to the topic sentence. In this lesson, we shall discuss other ways to develop a paragraph by adding detailed information that relates to the topic sentence. We can support a topic sentence by adding definitions, examples, facts, anecdotes, arguments, and analogies. These methods of building paragraphs will be useful when we write other types of essays in later lessons.

Notice how we use these different methods to support the following topic sentence:

Travelers should clearly label their baggage.

Definitions   To explain the topic sentence, we can define a term or a concept. **Definitions** may help the reader to understand more fully the meaning of the topic sentence.

> Travelers should clearly label their baggage. *To label is to affix a gummed piece of paper, or tag, to an article in order to identify its contents or owner.*

Examples   An **example** is a sample or an illustration. In almost any kind of writing, examples help to clarify a topic sentence. They offer the reader evidence.

> Travelers should clearly label their baggage. *For example, using bright pink ribbon, my aunt ties a large name tag to her suitcase. This way she can easily recognize her own bag.*

Facts   A **fact** is a piece of information that can be proved to be true. It is a *fact*, for example, that Alaska is the largest state in the Union. An *opinion*, on the other hand, is a judgment or belief. That Alaska is the most beautiful state in the Union is an *opinion*. It cannot be proved. Below, we add a fact to support the topic sentence.

Travelers should clearly label their baggage. *The Fourth-Street Bus Station loses an average of six pieces of unmarked luggage every week day.*

Anecdotes   To entertain the reader while illustrating our point, we can write an **anecdote,** a short account of an incident, something that happened to us or to someone we know, which relates to the topic sentence.

Travelers should clearly label their baggage. *As I began to unpack after my trip to Peru, I was shocked to find a suitcase full of diapers and baby clothes! Obviously, I had brought home someone else's bag and not my own.*

Arguments   In some kinds of writing, especially in persuasive writing, logical **arguments** can help to support our topic sentence. An argument might seek to disprove an opposing viewpoint.

Travelers should clearly label their baggage. *Some people think this is unnecessary, but it only takes a minute, and it can save travelers the frustration of losing their valuable possessions.*

Analogies   Sometimes we can use an **analogy** to clarify a point. An analogy is a comparison. To be effective, the two things being compared must have many similarities. Usually interesting to a reader, an analogy will help the reader to better understand the topic sentence.

Travelers should clearly label their baggage. *Without a name tag, a suitcase in the baggage claim area may be as difficult to find as a needle in a haystack.*

Practice   For a–f, use this topic sentence: *We need to clean our desks to prevent the accumulation of too much clutter.*

a. Write a *definition* that could be used to expand the topic sentence above.

b. Write an *example* that might follow the topic sentence above.

c. Write a *fact* to support the topic sentence.

d. Write an *anecdote* to illustrate the topic sentence.

      Student Workbook, 9781419098550

e. Write an *argument* that might prove the topic sentence.

f. Write an *analogy*, or comparison, to clarify the topic sentence.

Additional Practice Using the methods that you have learned in this lesson, expand each of the following topic sentences into a paragraph of at least five sentences.

1. Everyone can benefit from some kind of physical exercise.

2. Learning to save and budget money is an important step in becoming an adult.

3. A balanced diet is necessary for good health.

4. Sometimes advertisements deceive people.

5. Laughter is good medicine.

Four Purposes for Writing

Every piece of writing has a purpose. There are four basic purposes for writing: narrative, expository, descriptive, and persuasive.

Narrative writing tells a story or relates a series of events. A letter describing your five-day backpack trip in the High Sierras would be narrative writing. In Lesson 19, you will write a narrative essay telling about a personal experience of your choice.

Expository writing gives information or explains. A scientific article entitled "How a Microwave Works" is an example of expository writing. Your essay explaining that fireworks can be dangerous was also an example of expository writing.

Descriptive writing describes a person, place, or thing. Examples include a brochure describing beautiful Glacier Bay in Alaska, a personal composition about your favorite cousin, and a "Lost Dog" poster that tells exactly what the lost dog looks like. In Lesson 22, you will practice this type of writing by describing a person whom you can observe.

Persuasive writing attempts to convince someone to do or believe something. An advertisement for Tuff Cotton Balls, an article about the importance of saving an old oak tree from being uprooted by housing developers, and a campaign flyer urging voters to elect a certain candidate are all examples of persuasive writing.

The Persuasive Essay

Keeping in mind the structure of a complete essay described in Lesson 1, we shall prepare to write a persuasive essay using the following sentence as our thesis statement:

People should not be allowed to smoke in restaurants.

The goal of this essay will be to convince or *persuade* the reader that people should not be allowed to smoke in restaurants.

Persuasive essays usually deal with controversial topics, subjects that have two sides. If you prefer, you may argue the opposite side and rewrite the thesis statement to read, "People *should* be allowed to smoke in restaurants."

Your essay will prove that your thesis statement is correct. You will convince the reader of this.

Brainstorming
Brainstorming is always our first step in writing an essay. Recall from Writing Lesson 2 that we draw a circle in the middle of a blank sheet of paper. Inside the circle, write the thesis statement. Then quickly begin to write in the area outside the circle any and all words that come into your mind as soon as they come into your mind.

- Write quickly, and do not worry about spelling or neatness.

- Write for about three minutes or until your paper is covered with words, whichever comes first.

Organizing your Ideas
After you have brainstormed, look at the ideas you have generated and identify the ones that best support your thesis statement. Follow these steps to organize your ideas:

1. Take a moment to look at the words or groups of words you wrote. Some of them will begin to stand out as relating very well to the thesis; they will firmly argue your point and convince the reader. Others will begin to look as though they don't belong or are not as strong.

2. Choose at least three different words or groups of words that best support the thesis. Circle them. If you cannot decide on just three, you may circle four or five. If you circle more than three words or groups of words, you have more than enough support for your thesis statement. You can write several body paragraphs of support, or you might later decide to combine one or more arguments or to eliminate the weaker ones.

3. These circled word groups will become your body paragraph ideas. Write these ideas on a separate piece of paper leaving space underneath each idea to add more notes later for expanding the paragraphs.

4. Look at your body paragraph ideas and try to determine the order in which they should be arranged in the body of your essay to best support your thesis. Number the ideas. You can rearrange the order or even eliminate or add additional body paragraphs at any time as ideas come to you.

Forming Topic Sentences Once you have selected the best ideas from your brainstorming and placed them on a separate page, take those ideas and form them into topic sentences. Each topic sentence will become a main idea for your essay's body paragraphs.

Practice Write at least three topic sentences that clearly support your thesis statement. Keep this assignment in your folder or binder. In Lesson 7, we shall develop these topic sentences into body paragraphs and then complete the persuasive essay.

Writing the Persuasive Essay

In Lesson 6, you prepared to write your persuasive essay. By brainstorming, you gathered ideas. You chose the best of those ideas and put them in the order that best supports your thesis statement. Then you used the ideas to create at least three topic sentences. Now you are ready to write the complete essay.

Practice Using the topic sentences you wrote for Lesson 6, follow the steps below to complete the persuasive essay.

1. For each topic sentence, write a body paragraph to support the thesis statement. Refer back to Lesson 5 for different ways to expand a topic sentence into a paragraph. In addition to experience and opinion sentences, you might write definitions, examples, facts, anecdotes, arguments, or analogies that support the topic sentence.

2. Create an introductory paragraph and a concluding paragraph. Remember that the introductory sentence should grab the reader's interest and that the "last words" of your conclusion will leave a lasting impression.

3. Add transitions between body paragraphs to make your ideas easier for the reader to follow. Pay special attention to the transition into the concluding paragraph.

4. Finally, put all the parts together to form a complete essay. As you are working, make any necessary corrections to your previous work. You might add things, take things out, or make any other change that results in a more convincing, persuasive essay.

Additional Practice (Optional) After you have evaluated your persuasive essay using the guidelines in Lesson 8, you might try writing another persuasive essay on one of these topics, choosing "should" or "should not" to complete your thesis statement:

1. Our school day (should, should not) be shortened by one hour.

2. The federal government (should, should not) spend more money funding research for the cure of cancer.

3. California home owners (should, should not) be allowed to remove healthy oak trees from their property.

4. Mountain lions (should, should not) be allowed to roam free in areas where people live.

5. People (should, should not) have to pay a fee to camp in the National Forest.

6. High-school students (should, should not) be allowed to wear whatever they want to school.

7. Fourteen-year-olds (should, should not) be allowed to drive.

Evaluating the Persuasive Essay

We have learned that all of the writing we do is "work in progress." The knowledge that *writing is a process* guides our thinking throughout the construction of an essay. From the first steps in organizing our thoughts, to creating body paragraphs, to adding transitions, we constantly make changes to improve our work.

At each step of the writing process, we should stop to reevaluate both our thoughts and the words we have placed on the page.

Evaluating Your Writing

In Lesson 7, you completed your persuasive essay. Now that some time has passed, you are ready to evaluate it using the following guidelines.

Ask yourself these questions:

- Is my introductory sentence interesting? *If it is not interesting to you, it certainly will not be interesting to the reader.*

- Does my thesis statement clearly state my position?

- Does each body paragraph have a clear topic sentence at the beginning that tells the reader exactly what the paragraph will be about? *Read each topic sentence without the rest of the paragraph to see if it can stand alone as a strong idea.*

- Does each of my topic sentences strongly support my thesis statement?

- Are there other personal experiences, facts, examples, arguments, anecdotes, or analogies, that I can add to help improve my credibility and help the reader to better understand my point?

- Have I described in my opinion sentences my emotions and feeling so well that they create a picture in the mind of the reader to help him or her feel the same as I feel?

- Does each paragraph (except for the first) begin with an effective transition?

- Are there other arguments that I can add as additional body paragraphs to help me prove my point?

- Are some of my arguments weak and unconvincing? Should they be removed because they do not help me prove my point?

- Do my body paragraphs appear in the best possible order to prove my point? Could I place them in a different order that is more logical or effective?

- Is each sentence constructed as well as it should be? *Read each sentence in each paragraph as if it were the only sentence on the page. This helps you to catch sentence fragments, run-on sentences, misspellings, and grammatical errors.*

- Does my concluding paragraph summarize and reinforce the ideas and opinions expressed in the essay? Have I convinced the reader that my thesis statement is true?

Practice   Use the Evaluation Form on the page following this lesson to evaluate the persuasive essay you wrote for Lesson 7. Read your essay carefully as you check for the items listed on the Evaluation Form. Write YES or NO in the blank next to each question.

When you are finished, you will either be confident that you have a strong essay, or you will know where it needs to be improved.

If you answered NO to one or more of the questions on the Evaluation Form, rewrite to improve those areas.

When you can answer YES to every question on the Evaluation Form, you will have completed this assignment.

Persuasive Essay Evaluation Form

Thesis: _____

_____ Is my introductory sentence interesting? *If it is not interesting to you, it certainly won't be interesting to the reader.*

_____ Do I have a thesis statement that clearly explains the subject of this essay?

_____ Does my thesis statement clearly state my position?

_____ Does each body paragraph have a clear topic sentence at the beginning that tells the reader exactly what the paragraph will be about? *Read each topic sentence without the rest of the paragraph to see if it can stand alone as a strong idea.*

_____ Are there no other experiences, facts, or examples that I can add to help improve my credibility and help the reader to better understand my point?

_____ In my opinion sentences, have I described my emotions and feelings so well that they create a picture in the mind of the reader to help him or her feel the same as I feel?

_____ Does each paragraph (except for the first paragraph) begin with an effective transition?

_____ Are there no other arguments that I can add as additional body paragraphs to help me prove my point?

_____ Are all of my arguments strong and convincing?

_____ Do my body paragraphs appear in the best possible order to prove my point?

_____ Is each sentence structured as well as it could be? *Read each sentence in each paragraph as if it were the only sentence on the page. This helps you catch fragments and run-on sentences and evaluate the overall strength or weakness of each sentence.*

_____ Does my concluding paragraph summarize and reinforce the ideas and opinions expressed in the essay?

Writing a Strong Thesis Statement

The thesis statement clearly tells what the entire essay is about. We have practiced writing a complete essay based on an assigned thesis statement. In this lesson, we shall practice creating our own thesis statements for assigned topics.

We remember that the thesis statement not only tells the reader exactly what the essay is about but also clearly states the writer's position on the topic.

Brainstorming When faced with an assigned topic, we prepare by brainstorming in order to generate ideas and thoughts.

The first step in brainstorming is choosing your direction. You would not get into a car and just begin to drive, expecting to arrive at nowhere in particular. You need to know where you are going before you pull out of the driveway. In other words, you must think about the topic, choose your direction or focus, and prepare to define what your essay is about.

For example, if the assignment is to write about the qualities that make a good friend, your thesis statement could begin, "The qualities that make a good friend are …"

After brainstorming about the topic, perhaps you have decided that there are four specific qualities that make a good friend. If so, your thesis statement might be the following:

There are four important qualities that make a good friend.

Practice Below are ten topics that could be given to you as subjects for essays. For each topic, brainstorm briefly. Then write a declarative sentence that could be used as a strong thesis statement for a complete essay.

1. The best things about vacations from school

2. The things you like best about school

3. Why a person should learn a foreign language

4. Things that you would like to change about yourself

5. What you will do differently as a student this year from what you did last year

6. Some ways that you can help to make the world a better place

7. Some events you'll always remember

8. What you can do to improve or maintain your physical health

9. Some skills you would like to acquire

10. Kinds of things that make you happy

Preparing to Write an Expository Essay

The purpose of expository writing is to inform or explain. Expository writing tells why or how. The following might be titles for expository essays:

"How to Grow Delicious Turnips"

"New Burglar Alarm Technology"

"Where to Shop for Antiques"

"Why the Tortoise Makes a Good Pet"

"Building a Bird House from Scrap Lumber"

A good expository essay is well organized and clear. It might offer an explanation of how something works, information about a specific subject, or instructions for doing something.

In this lesson, we shall prepare to write an expository essay that explains how to wash a car.

Our goal is to write easy-to-follow instructions, which will require a detailed description of the process. Therefore, we shall break down the actions and carefully sequence them in a logical or practical order so that the reader can understand our step-by-step method of washing a car inside and out.

Brainstorming In order to generate thoughts and ideas, we shall brainstorm before creating a thesis statement for our *how-to* essay.

• Write quickly, and do not worry about spelling or neatness.

• Write for about three minutes or until your paper is covered with words, whichever comes first.

Writing a Thesis Statement Now it is time to state the purpose of your essay in a clear thesis statement. Using the ideas you have written by brainstorming, write a sentence that tells what your essay is about. Hint: Will you be presenting a certain number of *steps* in your how-to essay? Or will you be explaining a number of different *ways* to wash a car? Your thesis statement will reveal your presentation plan.

Organizing your Ideas

After you have written a strong thesis statement telling what your essay is about, look at the ideas you have generated by brainstorming and identify the ones that best support your thesis statement. When writing an expository essay, it is sometimes helpful to make an outline to help you organize your ideas. For example, your outline might look something like this:

How to Wash a Car

I. Preparation
    A. Appropriate dress
        1. Old clothes
        2. Shoes that water won't ruin
    B. Materials
        1. Bucket of soapy water
        2. Hose
        3. Towels

II. Process
    A. Cleaning inside of car
        1. Vacuuming
        2. Washing windows
        3. Deodorizing
    B. Cleaning outside of car
        1. Soaping
        2. Scrubbing
        3. Rinsing
        4. Drying
    C. Cleaning special parts of car
        1. Tires
        2. Mirrors and windows
        3. Chrome

III. Afterward
    A. Clean-up of towels, buckets, hose, etc.
    B. How the car should look and smell

For this assignment, you may either use the outline above, or you may create your own outline or thought clusters based on the ideas you generated while brainstorming. If you choose to use an outline, each Roman numeral part of your outline will represent a body paragraph to be developed later. You should have at least three of these.

Tone   The **tone** of an essay reflects the writer's attitude toward the topic. Your attitude can be formal or informal, sarcastic or straight-forward, serious or silly, admiring or critical. Before you begin writing, you must decide on your tone.

Forming Topic Sentences   Once you have decided on your tone, selected the main ideas from your brainstorming, and arranged them in clusters or an outline, take those ideas and form them into topic sentences. Each topic sentence will become a main idea for your essay's body paragraphs.

Practice   Write a thesis statement and at least three topic sentences that clearly explain your thesis statement. Keep this assignment in your folder or binder. In Lesson 11, we shall develop these topic sentences into body paragraphs and then complete the expository essay.

Writing the Expository Essay

In Lesson 10, you prepared to write your expository essay about how to wash a car. By brainstorming, you gathered ideas and wrote a thesis statement. You chose the best of those ideas and put them into clusters or an outline to create a logical order, or organization, for your presentation. Then you used the main ideas to create at least three topic sentences. Now you are ready to write the complete essay.

Practice Using the topic sentences you wrote for Lesson 10, follow the steps below to complete the expository essay.

1. For each topic sentence, write a body paragraph to support the thesis statement. Refer to your notes or outline and use the ideas underneath each Roman numeral to write body sentences that further explain, or expand, each topic sentence.

2. Create an introductory paragraph and a concluding paragraph. Remember that the introductory sentence should grab the reader's interest and that the "last words" of your conclusion will leave a lasting impression.

3. Add transitions between body paragraphs to make your ideas easier for the reader to follow. Transitions that indicate order, such as "the first step…" or "the second step…," are appropriate in a how-to essay. Pay special attention to the transition into the concluding paragraph.

4. Finally, put all the parts together to form a complete essay. As you are working, make any necessary corrections to your previous work. You might add things, take things out, or make any other change that results in a clearer, easier-to-follow expository essay.

Additional Practice (Optional) After you have evaluated your expository essay using the guidelines in Lesson 12, you might try writing another expository essay on a topic of your choice or on one of these topics:

1. Explain how to play a game, any game with which you are familiar.

2. Write an essay giving at least three reasons why your school is the best in the country.

3. Introduce your reader to an interesting person, such as one of your relatives, family members, or friends.

4. Write an essay about the proper care and feeding of an animal that you are familiar with.

5. Read about cowbirds and then write an essay explaining how they are different from other small birds.

6. Compare and contrast the alligator and the crocodile.

Evaluating the Expository Essay

We remember that all of our writing is "work in progress." The knowledge that *writing is a process* guides our thinking throughout the construction of an essay. Throughout the steps of brainstorming, organizing our thoughts, creating body paragraphs, and adding transitions, we constantly make changes to improve our work.

Evaluating Your Writing

In Lesson 11, you completed your expository essay. Now that some time has passed, you are ready to evaluate it using the following guidelines.

Ask yourself these questions:

- Is my introductory sentence interesting? *If it is not interesting to you, it certainly will not be interesting to the reader.*

- Does my thesis statement clearly state what my essay is about?

- Does each body paragraph have a clear topic sentence at the beginning that tells the reader exactly what the paragraph will be about? *Read each topic sentence without the rest of the paragraph to see if it can stand alone as a strong idea.*

- Does each of my topic sentences strongly support my thesis statement?

- Are there other details, facts, examples, or steps, that I can add to help improve my explanation or help the reader to better follow my instructions?

- Are my sentences in a logical or practical order?

- Does each paragraph (except for the first) begin with an effective transition?

- Are there other details that I can add as additional body paragraphs to create a fuller or clearer explanation?

- Are some of my sentences weak or confusing? Should they be removed because they do not help me to explain?

- Do my body paragraphs appear in the best possible order? Could I place them in a different order that is more logical or effective?

- Is each sentence constructed as well as it should be? *Read each sentence in each paragraph as if it were the only sentence on the page. This helps you to catch sentence fragments, run-on sentences, misspellings, and grammatical errors.*

- Does my concluding paragraph summarize and reinforce the ideas expressed in the essay?

Practice   Use the Evaluation Form on the page following this lesson to evaluate the expository essay you wrote for Lesson 11. Read your essay carefully as you check for the items listed on the Evaluation Form. Write YES or NO in the blank next to each question.

When you are finished, you will either be confident that you have a strong essay, or you will know where it needs to be improved.

If you answered NO to one or more of the questions on the Evaluation Form, rewrite to improve those areas.

When you can answer YES to every question on the Evaluation Form, you will have completed this assignment.

Expository Essay Evaluation Form

Thesis: _____

_____ Is my introductory sentence interesting? *If it is not interesting to you, it certainly won't be interesting to the reader.*

_____ Do I have a thesis statement that clearly explains the subject of this essay?

_____ Does my thesis statement clearly state my method of presentation?

_____ Does each body paragraph have a clear topic sentence at the beginning that tells the reader exactly what the paragraph will be about? *Read each topic sentence without the rest of the paragraph to see if it can stand alone as a strong idea.*

_____ Have I included every detail, fact, or example that I can to help improve my explanation and help the reader to better understand my point?

_____ Within each paragraph, are my sentences in a logical or practical order?

_____ Does each paragraph (except for the first paragraph) begin with an effective transition?

_____ Are there no other ideas that I can add as additional body paragraphs to create a fuller or clearer explanation?

_____ Are all of my sentences strong and clear? Do they all help me to explain?

_____ Do my body paragraphs appear in the best possible order? Is their order logical and effective?

_____ Is each sentence structured as well as it could be? *Read each sentence in each paragraph as if it were the only sentence on the page. This helps you catch fragments and run-on sentences and evaluate the overall strength or weakness of each sentence.*

_____ Does my concluding paragraph summarize and reinforce the ideas expressed in the essay?

Developing an Outline

We have learned that an outline can help us to organize our ideas for an expository essay. In an outline, we can arrange and sequence thoughts in a logical manner.

In this lesson, we shall review the basic outline form and practice developing an outline from an essay we have already written. This exercise will give us confidence in our ability to make an outline in preparation for writing future essays or research papers.

Outline Form An **outline** is a list of topics and subtopics arranged in an organized form. We use Roman numerals for main topics. For subtopics, we use uppercase letters. For a very detailed outline we use alternating numbers and letters as shown below.

Title

I. Main topic

  A. Subtopic of I

  B. Subtopic of I

    1. Subtopic of B

    2. Subtopic of B

      a. Subtopic of 2

      b. Subtopic of 2

        (1) Subtopic of b

        (2) Subtopic of b

          (a) Subtopic of (2)

          (b) Subtopic of (2)

II. Main topic

  A. Etc.

    1. Etc.

Notice that we indent subtopics so that all letters or numbers of the same kind will come directly under one another in a vertical line.

Topic Outline An outline may be either a topic outline or a sentence outline. In a **topic outline** each main topic or subtopic is written as a single word or phrase. Below is an example of a topic outline of the first part of an essay on objections to homework.

Homework Hassles

I. Why homework is necessary
    A. To learn new things
    B. To practice skills

II. Why some homework is irritating
    A. Too repetitious
    B. Too time-consuming

Sentence Outline In a **sentence outline** each topic is expressed as a complete sentence. Notice how the sentence outline below communicates more meaning than the short phrases of the topic outline.

Homework Hassles

I. Homework is necessary.
    A. We learn new things as we do our homework.
    B. Homework provides practice that increases skills.

II. Some homework is irritating.
    A. Too much repetition is irritating.
    B. Homework that consumes much time is irritating.

Practice On a separate sheet of paper, practice the outlining process by organizing the following set of information in a topic outline form. First, look carefully over the list. You will find *one* main topic (I.) and *three* subtopics (A., B., and C.). The rest of the items will be sub-subtopics, or subtopics of subtopics (1., 2., 3.,…). You might begin by circling the main topic and underlining the three subtopics. You may work with your teacher or with a group of students for this project.

The completed outline (answer) for this Practice is found on the last page of the Writing packet.

exclamation mark	period
subject	noun
grammatical terms	parts of speech
comma	semicolon
pronoun	parts of a sentence
predicate	adjective

preposition	direct object
colon	dash
punctuation marks	verb
adverb	question mark
interjection	conjunction
quotation marks	indirect object

Additional Practice For Lesson 3, you wrote a complete essay containing at least three body paragraphs. Create a topic outline covering the body paragraphs of that essay. Hint: The topic sentence of each body paragraph will become a word or phrase beside a Roman numeral indicating a main topic in your outline. Therefore, your outline will have at least three Roman numerals.

Additional Practice (Optional) For Lesson 7, you wrote a persuasive essay containing at least three body paragraphs. Create a topic outline for this essay.

Preparing to Write a Research Paper: The Working Bibliography

A research paper is a type of expository writing based on information gathered from a variety of reliable sources. In the future, you may be asked to write a research paper for an English, history, science, art, or music class. Knowing the procedure for writing a good research paper will help you to become a successful high school and college student.

In this lesson, we shall learn how to prepare for writing a research paper on an assigned subject. To practice the procedure, you may choose one of the following subjects:

1. The Opossum, a Good Neighbor

2. How the Internet Got Started

3. Isaac Newton's Contribution to Our Understanding of Color

4. How to Avoid Botulism When Canning Pickles

5. A subject suggested by your teacher

Tone The research paper requires a serious tone. The writing should be formal and impersonal. Therefore, we do not use first person pronouns, such as *I, me,* or *my.*

Gathering Sources of Information The first step in researching your subject is to compile a **working bibliography,** a collection of possible sources of information. Consider the following possibilities for your research:

- library research aids including card catalog, *Readers' Guide*, and reference works

- internet

- government publications

- personal interviews or correspondence

- museums

- scholarly journals

Evaluating Sources of Information

Not all sources are reliable or useful. We must evaluate each source for its usefulness. Asking the following questions will help us to evaluate each source:

1. *Is the information current?* A 1970 study of smog in large cities is out-of-date. Therefore, it would not be an appropriate source for a paper on today's pollution problems except for drawing comparisons with the past.

2. *Is the source objective and impartial?* An article written by the president of Mountain Spring Bottled Water about impurities in local well water might not be an objective source. The author could be trying to sell you something.

3. *For what audience was the source intended?* Material written for young children might be over-simplified while material written for specialists might be too technical.

Preparing Bibliography Cards

After gathering sources, evaluating each one for its usefulness, and choosing only those that are appropriate, we are ready to compile a working bibliography, the list of sources from which we will glean information for our research paper. Using three-by-five inch index cards, we record each source on a separate card. We include all the information listed below, for we will need it to prepare our final Bibliography when our paper is completed.

BOOKS

1. Author's (or editor's) full name, last name first. Indicate editor by placing *ed.* after the name. If the book has more than one author, only the first author is written last name first. Others are written first name first.

2. Title and subtitle underlined

3. City of publication

4. Publisher's name

5. Most recent copyright year.

MAGAZINE, NEWSPAPER, JOURNAL, AND ENCYCLOPEDIA ARTICLES

1. Author's (or editor's) full name, last name first. Indicate editor by placing <u>ed.</u> after the name. If the article has more than one author, only the first author is written last name first. Others are written first name first.

2. Title of article in quotation marks

3. Name of magazine, newspaper, journal, or encyclopedia underlined

4. Date and page numbers of *magazines*
   Date, edition, section, page numbers of *newspapers*
   Volume, year, page numbers of *journals*
   Edition and year of *encyclopedias*

We assign each bibliography card a "source number" and write it in the upper left corner. Later we will use this number to identify the sources of our notes. Below are some sample bibliography cards.

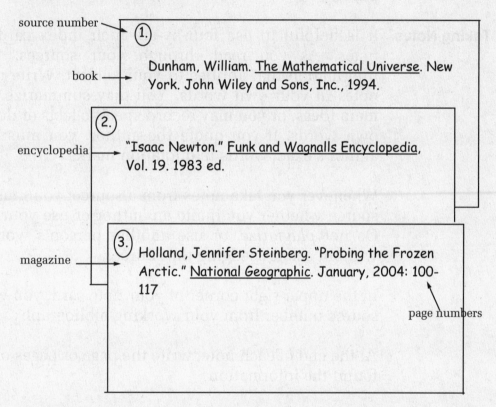

source number

(1.)

book → Dunham, William. The Mathematical Universe. New York. John Wiley and Sons, Inc., 1994.

(2.)

encyclopedia → "Isaac Newton." Funk and Wagnalls Encyclopedia, Vol. 19. 1983 ed.

(3.)

magazine → Holland, Jennifer Steinberg. "Probing the Frozen Arctic." National Geographic. January, 2004: 100-117

page numbers

Practice After you have chosen a subject from the list of suggestions for your research paper, follow the instructions in this lesson for gathering and evaluating sources and for preparing bibliography cards. Locate at least *four* appropriate sources and prepare a bibliography card for each one. Remember to assign each card a source number and write it in the upper left corner.

LESSON 15

Preparing to Write a Research Paper: Notes, Thesis, Outline

In Lesson 14, you chose a subject for a research paper and created a working bibliography, at least four sources of information that you will use for your paper. In this lesson, you will take notes from these sources, organize your notes, create a thesis statement, and develop an outline for your paper.

Taking Notes
It is helpful to use four-by-six inch index cards for taking notes. As you read through your sources, write down information that applies to your subject. Write most of your notes in your own words. You may summarize the author's main ideas, or you may record specific facts or details in your own words. If you quote the author, you must enclose the author's exact words in quotation marks.

Whenever you take notes from a source, you must credit that source whether you quote an author or use your own words. Do not *plagiarize*, or use another person's words or ideas, without acknowledging the source.

In the upper right corner of your note card, you will enter the source number from your working bibliography.

At the end of each note, write the page or pages on which you found the information.

Below is a sample note card.

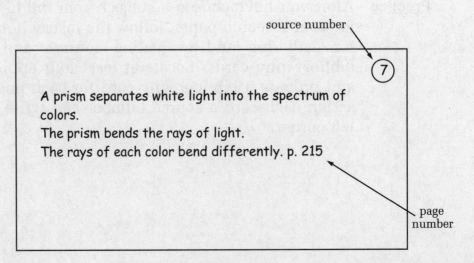

source number

⑦

A prism separates white light into the spectrum of colors.
The prism bends the rays of light.
The rays of each color bend differently. p. 215

page number

Organizing Your Information After you have taken notes on all your sources and gathered sufficient information for your research paper, take some time to organize your note cards and arrange them in a logical order.

Thesis Statement Now look over your organized notes and write a thesis statement that clearly explains the main idea of your research paper.

Outline In Lesson 13, you learned to develop an outline. Use your organized note cards to help you create an informal topic outline for your research paper. This outline will guide you as you begin to write the first draft of your paper in the next lesson.

Practice Follow the instructions in this lesson for taking notes from your sources. Then organize your notes, write a thesis statement, and develop an outline for your research paper.

LESSON 16

Writing the Research Paper

In Lesson 15, you took notes from your sources, organized your notes, wrote a thesis statement, and created an outline for your research paper.

Writing the First Draft

With your outline, your thesis statement, your notes, and your bibliography cards in front of you, you are ready to begin writing the first draft of your research paper. A first draft is a rough copy that is for your use only. It is meant to be revised again and again until you are satisfied with it.

As you write, keep in mind your thesis statement, your purpose, and the need for a formal tone. Use the information on your note cards to support your thesis and to fill in the details as you follow your outline for organization.

Create an introductory paragraph that captures the reader's attention. Consider beginning with a question, an interesting statement, an anecdote, or an example. Make certain that your opening paragraph includes your thesis statement.

Use the main points in your outline to create topic sentences for your body paragraphs. Then develop these topic sentences into paragraphs, making sure that all of your information relates to your thesis statement.

Pay special attention to transitions as you begin each new paragraph.

Your concluding paragraph will summarize and reinforce the ideas set forth in the rest of your research paper.

Documentation of Sources

Writing the first draft of a research paper involves bringing together information from your different sources, which you must acknowledge properly. We call this acknowledgement the **documentation** of sources.

As you write, you must credit your sources for both ideas and quotations. There are various methods of documenting sources for research papers. In this book, we shall practice a method called *parenthetical citations*. This form identifies sources in parentheses that are placed as close as possible to the ideas or quotations we are citing. Inside the parentheses, we place a reference to the source in our Bibliography, which is found at the end of the research paper.

Usually, the reference inside the parentheses consists only of an author's last name and the page number from which the material was taken. For example, (McKeever 42) would appear right after an idea taken from page forty-two in John McKeever's book, which is listed in the Bibliography.

When no author and only a title is given for a source, we place a shortened form of the title and the page number or numbers in the parentheses: ("Black Holes" 215-217).

Notice that the end punctuation for a sentence containing borrowed material is placed *after* the parenthetical citation:

> The pulling power of black holes is so strong that even light cannot escape from them (McKeever 42).

punctuation mark

The highly respected Modern Language Association (MLA) gives us many more detailed guidelines for parenthetical citations. However, in this lesson we shall follow the simplified instructions above.

The Bibliography The Bibliography, the list of the sources that you used as you wrote your paper, comes at the end of the research paper.

Follow these steps to create your Bibliography:

1. Alphabetize your bibliography cards according to the last names of the authors or the first important word in a title if there is no author.

2. Copy the information from all of your alphabetized bibliography cards under the title "Bibliography" or "Works Cited."

3. Indent all lines after the first line of each entry and punctuate as shown in the example below.

Bibliography

Grim, Edmund. "Six Ways to Clean the Sewer." Home and Grounds Journal, July, 1999: 12-15.

Leadfoot, Doris. A Study in Dynamics. New York, Grassvale Publishers, 2001.

In high school and college, you will learn to follow more detailed guidelines given by MLA for bibliographic entries. However, in this lesson you may follow the simplified instructions above unless your teacher advises you to do otherwise.

Practice   Follow the procedure given in this lesson for writing the first draft of your research paper, documenting your sources, and making your Bibliography.

Evaluating the Research Paper

The knowledge that *writing is a process* guides our thinking throughout the construction of our research paper. From the first steps in choosing our subject, to gathering information and organizing our thoughts, to creating body paragraphs, to adding transitions, we constantly make changes to improve our work.

Evaluating Your Writing

In Lesson 16, you completed the first draft of your research paper. Now that some time has passed, you are ready to evaluate it using the following guidelines.

Ask yourself these questions:

- Are my sources reliable, objective, and current?

- Is my introductory sentence interesting? *If it is not interesting to you, it certainly will not be interesting to the reader.*

- Does my thesis clearly state the purpose of my paper?

- Does the beginning of the research paper clearly establish a formal, serious tone?

- Does each Body Paragraph have a clear topic sentence at the beginning that tells the reader exactly what the paragraph will be about? *Read each topic sentence without the rest of the paragraph to see if it can stand alone as a strong idea.*

- Does each paragraph include specific details and examples from my research?

- Have I correctly documented each piece of borrowed information?

- Are my sentences in a logical order?

- Does each paragraph (except for the first) begin with an effective transition?

- Are there other details that I can add as additional body paragraphs to create a fuller or more complete paper?

- Are some of my sentences weak or confusing? Should they be removed because they do not relate to my thesis?

- Do my body paragraphs appear in the best possible order? Could I place them in a different order that is more logical or effective?

- Is each sentence constructed as well as it should be? *Read each sentence in each paragraph as if it were the only sentence on the page. This helps you to catch sentence fragments, run-on sentences, misspellings, and grammatical errors.*

- Does my ending paragraph obviously conclude my presentation? Does it reinforce my thesis statement?

Practice Use the Evaluation Form on the page following this lesson to evaluate the research paper you wrote for Lesson 16. Read your research paper carefully as you check for the items listed on the Evaluation Form. Write YES or NO in the blank next to each question.

When you are finished, you will either be confident that you have a strong research paper, or you will know where it needs to be improved.

If you answered NO to one or more of the questions on the Evaluation Form, rewrite to improve those areas.

When you can answer YES to every question on the Evaluation Form, you will have completed this assignment.

Research Paper Evaluation Form

Subject: _____

_____ Are my sources reliable, objective, and current?

_____ Is my introductory sentence interesting? *If it is not interesting to you, it certainly will not be interesting to the reader.*

_____ Does the beginning of the research paper clearly establish a formal, serious tone?

_____ Does the thesis clearly state the purpose of the paper?

_____ Does each body paragraph have a clear topic sentence at the beginning that tells the reader exactly what the paragraph will be about? *Read each topic sentence without the rest of the paragraph to see if it can stand alone as a strong idea.*

_____ Do the details all contribute to the reader's understanding of the thesis?

_____ Within each paragraph, are my sentences in a logical or practical order?

_____ Does each paragraph (except for the first paragraph) begin with an effective transition?

_____ Is each piece of borrowed material properly documented? Have I credited each of my sources?

_____ Are all of my sentences strong and clear? Do they all directly relate to the thesis?

_____ Do my body paragraphs appear in the best possible order? Is their order logical and effective?

_____ Is each sentence structured as well as it could be? *Read each sentence in each paragraph as if it were the only sentence on the page. This helps you catch fragments and run-on sentences and evaluate the overall strength or weakness of each sentence.*

_____ Does my concluding paragraph summarize my research and reinforce my thesis statement?

LESSON 18

Preparing to Write a Personal Narrative

Personal Narrative

Narrative writing tells a story or relates a series of events. In a **personal narrative,** the writer tells a story about a significant personal experience or event.

In this lesson, you will prepare to write a personal narrative in which you will share your feelings about how an experience affected you or taught you something. Your first-person account might include action, suspense, dialogue, and vivid description.

Choosing a Personal Experience

To think of an experience for a personal narrative that you would like to share, consider the following:

- a wonderful (or disastrous) first time that you did something

- a memorable struggle or hardship that you experienced

- a "turning point" in your life

- an interesting, exciting, humorous, or moving event in your life

- an unusual or once-in-a-life-time experience, such as touring a distant country, meeting a famous person, or making an amazing discovery

Reading through the daily journals that you have written might give you additional ideas.

Brainstorming

On a piece of scratch paper, quickly write every experience that comes to your mind. When you have finished, select the one that you think is most interesting and write it on another piece of paper.

After selecting the experience you plan to write about in your personal narrative, begin brainstorming in order to recall details or emotions about this experience. List all words and phrases that come to mind. Without concern for spelling or grammar, write everything that occurs to you.

Organizing your Information Once you have gathered your thoughts and memories, begin to plan your narrative by organizing the events in a logical order, which might be chronological order—the sequence in which the events occurred. Your rough plan might look something like this:

First: My brother and I went hiking in Dark Canyon...

Then: We wandered off the main trail and...

Then: The sun went down and...

Then: We heard coyotes, wolves, and...

Finally: We learned how important it is to carry a compass and a flashlight.

Practice For your personal narrative, write a rough plan similar to the one above. In the next lesson, you will expand each part of this plan into a paragraph and complete your narrative by filling in detail, action, and dialogue.

LESSON 19

Writing a Personal Narrative

In Lesson 18, you chose an interesting personal experience and created a rough plan for writing a personal narrative. In this lesson, you will use your rough plan and any other notes and begin writing your narrative.

Opening Paragraph

Remember that your opening paragraph should capture the interest of the reader and establish your tone, which reveals your feelings or attitudes about the experience. You will write in first person, using the pronoun *I* or *we*.

Body Paragraphs

Although you have a plan to follow, you may alter it as you write. Following the opening paragraph, each "then" part of your rough plan might become the topic sentence for a body paragraph in which you fill in details, actions, and any necessary dialogue.

Concluding Paragraph

Your concluding paragraph will include a personal summary or commentary about how the experience affected you or taught you something significant.

Practice

Write your personal narrative according to the guidelines above. Include an opening paragraph, two or more body paragraphs, and a concluding paragraph.

Evaluating the Personal Narrative

All of our writing is "work in progress." The knowledge that *writing is a process* guides our thinking throughout the construction of our personal narrative. From the first steps in selecting an experience to share, to organizing our thoughts, to creating body paragraphs, to adding transitions, we constantly make changes to improve our work.

Evaluating Your Writing

In Lesson 19, you completed your personal narrative. Now that some time has passed, you are ready to evaluate it using the following guidelines.

Ask yourself these questions:

- Is my introductory sentence interesting? *If it is not interesting to you, it certainly will not be interesting to the reader.*

- Does the beginning of the narrative clearly establish the tone?

- Does each body paragraph have a clear topic sentence at the beginning that tells the reader exactly what the paragraph will be about? *Read each topic sentence without the rest of the paragraph to see if it can stand alone as a strong idea.*

- Is the first-person point of view consistently maintained throughout the narrative?

- Are there other details, descriptions, emotions, or dialogue I could add to make a more interesting narrative?

- Are my sentences in a logical or chronological order?

- Does each paragraph (except for the first) begin with an effective transition?

- Are there other details that I can add as additional body paragraphs to create a fuller or more complete narrative?

- Are some of my sentences weak or confusing? Should they be removed because they do not relate to the story?

- Do my body paragraphs appear in the best possible order? Could I place them in a different order that is more logical or effective?

- Is each sentence constructed as well as it should be? *Read each sentence in each paragraph as if it were the only sentence on the page. This helps you to catch sentence fragments, run-on sentences, misspellings, and grammatical errors.*

- Does my concluding paragraph contain a summary or commentary about how the experience affected me?

Practice Use the Evaluation Form on the page following this lesson to evaluate the personal narrative you wrote for Lesson 19. Read your narrative carefully as you check for the items listed on the Evaluation Form. Write YES or NO in the blank next to each question.

When you are finished, you will either be confident that you have a strong personal narrative, or you will know where it needs to be improved.

If you answered NO to one or more of the questions on the Evaluation Form, rewrite to improve those areas.

When you can answer YES to every question on the Evaluation Form, you will have completed this assignment.

Personal Narrative Evaluation Form

Title: _____

_____ Is my introductory sentence interesting? *If it is not interesting to you, it certainly won't be interesting to the reader.*

_____ Does the beginning of the narrative clearly establish the tone?

_____ Is the first-person point of view consistently maintained throughout the narrative?

_____ Does each body paragraph have a clear topic sentence at the beginning that tells the reader exactly what the paragraph will be about? *Read each topic sentence without the rest of the paragraph to see if it can stand alone as a strong idea.*

_____ Do the details all contribute to the reader's understanding of my personal experience?

_____ Within each paragraph, are my sentences in a logical or practical order?

_____ Does each paragraph (except for the first paragraph) begin with an effective transition?

_____ Are there no other details that I can add as additional body paragraphs to create a fuller or more complete narrative?

_____ Are all of my sentences strong and clear? Do they all directly relate to the story?

_____ Do my body paragraphs appear in the best possible order? Is their order logical and effective?

_____ Is each sentence structured as well as it could be? *Read each sentence in each paragraph as if it were the only sentence on the page. This helps you catch fragments and run-on sentences and evaluate the overall strength or weakness of each sentence.*

_____ Does my concluding paragraph contain a personal summary or commentary about how the experience affected me or taught me something?

Descriptive writing describes a person, place, object, or event. With language that appeals to the senses, descriptive writing creates pictures in the reader's mind. Strong, vivid, and precise words are essential in creating clear descriptions.

In this lesson, we shall discuss the use of modifiers, comparisons, and sensory expressions to create accurate and complete descriptions. Then you will prepare to write a descriptive essay about a person whom you can observe as you are writing.

Modifiers   To add detail, the we can use modifiers—adjectives and adverbs, phrases and clauses. Modifiers supply additional information, making nouns and verbs more specific and precise.

> *Fearless*, *flawless*, and *unflappable*, the super-hero stood *confidently* within arm's reach of the enemy.

Comparisons   In addition to adding modifiers, we can use comparisons to make a description more vivid. *Simile* and *metaphor* are two kinds of comparisons. A *simile* expresses similarity between two things by using the word *like* or *as*:

> *Like* a pogo stick, the border collie hopped over clumps of daisies in the meadow.

A *metaphor*, on the other hand, describes one thing as though it were another thing:

> She was springy and energetic, a *pogo stick* with fur.

Both comparisons, simile and metaphor, help the reader to see a fuller picture of the border collie.

Sensory Expressions   To create a more vivid image, we can appeal to the reader's five senses by detailing things that one can see, hear, smell, taste, and touch. For example, we can hear an engine *rumble*, see a snowflake *glisten*, smell the *perfume* of a rose, feel the *scratchiness* of a wool sweater, and taste the *tart* apple that makes our lips pucker.

Below, Washington Irving describes Ichabod Crane, the schoolmaster, in "The Legend of Sleepy Hollow."

> He was tall, but exceedingly lank, with narrow shoulders, long arms and legs, hands that dangled a mile out of his sleeves, feet that might have served for shovels, and his whole frame most loosely hung together. His head was small, and flat at top, with huge ears, large green glassy eyes, and a long snip nose, so that it looked like a weathercock perched upon his spindle neck, to tell which way the wind blew.

Irving's description demonstrates how a writer can use details, modifiers, and comparisons to give the reader a clear picture of an imaginary person.

In her novel *Johnny Tremain*, Esther Forbes uses metaphor and sensory images to describe a place:

> Boston slowly opened its eyes, stretched, and woke. The sun struck in horizontally from the east, flashing upon weathervanes—brass cocks and arrows, here a glass-eyed Indian, there a copper grasshopper—and the bells in the steeples cling-clanged, telling the people it was time to be up and about.

In the same novel, the author goes on to describe Johnny Tremain:

> Johnny was already in his leather breeches, pulling on his coarse shirt, tucking in the tails. He was a rather skinny boy, neither large nor small for fourteen. He had a thin, sleep-flushed face, light eyes, a wry mouth, and fair, lank hair. Although two years younger than the swinish Dove, inches shorter, pounds lighter, he knew, and old Mr. Lapham knew, busy Mrs. Lapham and her four daughters and Dove and Dusty also knew, that Johnny Tremain was boss of the attic, and almost of the house.

The examples above show how good authors create vivid pictures using details, modifiers, comparisons, and sensory expressions.

Brainstorming   After choosing one person whom you can observe as you write, you are ready to begin brainstorming in order to gather precise and concrete details that will appeal to the reader's senses and fully describe that person.

You might want to consider these aspects of the person:

1. Physical appearance—size, age, gender; colors, shapes, and textures of hair, eyes, skin, and clothing; peculiar features or facial expressions; movements and gestures;

2. Personality traits—mannerisms, habits, usual disposition. By their actions, people may demonstrate that they are intense or relaxed, hyperactive or laid-back, outgoing or shy, humble or proud, etc.

3. How the person affects others and the world around him or her—Where does the person live? What does the person do? What are his or her passions or interests? How does he or she relate to others? How does this person make you or other people feel?

On a blank piece of paper, quickly write everything that comes to your mind concerning the person you wish to describe. Without regard for spelling or grammar, write all the nouns, verbs, adjectives, adverbs, phrases, clauses, comparisons, and sensory expressions that occur to you.

Organizing your Information   Once you have gathered your thoughts and observations, begin to plan your descriptive essay by grouping the words and phrases into clusters. You might have one cluster of words and phrases that describe the person's physical appearance, another cluster focusing on the person's personality, and another telling about what the person does and/or how the person affects others and the world around him or her.

You can use each idea cluster to develop a topic sentence for each body paragraph in your essay.

Thesis Statement   In your essay, you will be describing many different aspects of one person. What is the main impression you want your reader to receive concerning this person? Your thesis statement will sum up that which is most important.

Practice   For your descriptive essay, write a thesis statement and three or more topic sentences about the person you wish to describe. In the next lesson, you will develop each topic sentence into a body paragraph by adding more detail. Keep your brainstorming paper and this assignment in your folder or binder so that you will be ready to complete your essay.

Writing a Descriptive Essay

In Lesson 21, you prepared to write your descriptive essay about a person of your choice. By brainstorming, you gathered ideas and details. Then you organized those details into clusters representing main ideas. From those clusters, you created a thesis statement and at least three topic sentences. Now you are ready to write the complete essay.

Practice Using the topic sentences you wrote for Lesson 21, follow the steps below to complete the expository essay.

1. Develop each topic sentence into a body paragraph, keeping your thesis in mind. Refer to your brainstorming notes and idea clusters to write body sentences that add more detail and create a vivid picture in the reader's mind.

2. Create an introductory paragraph and a concluding paragraph. Remember that the introductory sentence should grab the reader's interest and that the "last words" of your conclusion will leave a lasting impression.

3. Add transitions between body paragraphs to make your ideas easier for the reader to follow. Pay special attention to the transition into the concluding paragraph.

4. Finally, put all the parts together to form a complete essay. As you are working, make any necessary corrections to your previous work. You might add things, take things out, or make any other change that results in a clearer, fuller descriptive essay.

Additional Practice (Optional) After you have evaluated your descriptive essay using the guidelines in Lesson 23, you might try writing another descriptive essay on a topic of your choice or on one of these topics:

1. A character from a novel you have read

2. A room in your house or apartment

3. A pet, or an animal that interests you

4. An interesting or beautiful outdoor scene

5. A sporting event, birthday party, or other kind of celebration

LESSON 23

Evaluating the Descriptive Essay

Because *writing is a process* and all of our writing is "work in progress," we constantly make changes to improve our work.

Evaluating Your Writing

In Lesson 22, you completed your descriptive essay. Now that some time has passed, you are ready to evaluate it using the following guidelines.

Ask yourself these questions:

- Is my introductory sentence interesting? *If it is not interesting to you, it certainly will not be interesting to the reader.*

- Does the thesis statement focus on a single person, place, object, or event?

- Does the thesis statement give my main impression of the person, place, object, or event that I am describing?

- Does each body paragraph have a clear topic sentence at the beginning that tells the reader exactly what the paragraph will be about? *Read each topic sentence without the rest of the paragraph to see if it can stand alone as a strong idea.*

- Are there other details, modifiers, comparisons, or sensory expressions I could add to help the reader to visualize my topic?

- Are my sentences in a logical order?

- Does each paragraph (except for the first) begin with an effective transition?

- Are there other details that I can add as additional body paragraphs to create a fuller or more complete description?

- Are some of my sentences weak or confusing? Should they be removed because they do not relate to the topic?

- Do my body paragraphs appear in the best possible order? Could I place them in a different order that is more logical or effective?

- Is each sentence constructed as well as it should be? *Read each sentence in each paragraph as if it were the only sentence on the page. This helps you to catch sentence fragments, run-on sentences, misspellings, and grammatical errors.*

- Does my concluding paragraph sum up my main impression of the person, place, object, or event?

Practice Use the Evaluation Form on the page following this lesson to evaluate the descriptive essay you wrote for Lesson 22. Read your descriptive essay carefully as you check for the items listed on the Evaluation Form. Write YES or NO in the blank next to each question.

When you are finished, you will either be confident that you have a strong descriptive essay, or you will know where it needs to be improved.

If you answered NO to one or more of the questions on the Evaluation Form, rewrite to improve those areas.

When you can answer YES to every question on the Evaluation Form, you will have completed this assignment.

Descriptive Essay Evaluation Form

Topic: _____

_____ Is my introductory sentence interesting? *If it is not interesting to you, it certainly won't be interesting to the reader.*

_____ Does the thesis statement focus on a single person, place, object, or event?

_____ Does the thesis statement give my main impression of that person, place, object, or event?

_____ Does each body paragraph have a clear topic sentence at the beginning that tells the reader exactly what the paragraph will be about? *Read each topic sentence without the rest of the paragraph to see if it can stand alone as a strong idea.*

_____ Do the details all contribute to the reader's ability to visualize or mentally experience my topic?

_____ Within each paragraph, are my sentences in a logical order?

_____ Does each paragraph (except for the first paragraph) begin with an effective transition?

_____ Have I used enough modifiers, comparisons, and sensory expressions to enable the reader to visualize my topic?

_____ Are all of my sentences strong and clear? Do they all directly relate to the topic?

_____ Do my body paragraphs appear in the best possible order? Is their order logical and effective?

_____ Is each sentence structured as well as it could be? *Read each sentence in each paragraph as if it were the only sentence on the page. This helps you catch fragments and run-on sentences and evaluate the overall strength or weakness of each sentence.*

_____ Does my concluding paragraph sum up my main impression of my topic?

Preparing to Write an Imaginative Story

We have practiced writing vivid descriptions of people, places, objects, or events using details, modifiers, comparisons, and sensory expressions. We have also written a personal narrative with dialogue, logical sentence order, and effective transitions. In this lesson, we shall use all the writing skills we have learned so far in order to create our own imaginative story.

An imaginative story is fiction; it is not a true story although it may be based on something that really happened.

Conflict, characters, setting, and plot are all parts of the imaginative story. In preparing to write our story, we shall gather information concerning each of these parts.

Conflict A short story must have a problem or situation in which struggle occurs. A character may be in conflict with another character, with the forces of nature, with the rules of society, or even with his or her own self, as an internal conflict brought about by pangs of conscience or feelings of ambivalence.

For example, notice the possible conflicts related to the two situations below.

SITUATION 1: A drought hits a farming community.
Conflict: Some farmers steal water from others to keep their crops from dying.
Conflict: Local government officials try to enforce water rationing.

SITUATION 2: The substitute teacher has fallen asleep during the class's silent reading period.
Conflict: Some students want to take advantage of the situation and misbehave while others want to continue their silent reading.
Conflict: One student worries that the class will be punished for misbehavior.
Conflict: One student is embarrassed, for the sleeping substitute teacher is his aunt!

To find a situation and conflict for your own imaginative story, you might talk to friends or family members, watch the news, read the newspaper, or observe what is happening in the lives of people around you.

In preparation for story-writing, spend several minutes brainstorming with the help of a friend, teacher, or family member to gather ideas of situations and conflicts. Write down all the situations and possible resulting conflicts that come to mind. Then choose the one conflict that most interests you for your imaginative story.

Tone Your attitude toward the conflict will create the **tone** of your story. The details and language you use might evoke joy, fear, amusement, grief, or some other emotion. For example, you will want your story to make the reader laugh if you feel that the situation facing the characters is funny. On the other hand, if you feel that the situation is serious and worrisome, you will try to increase the reader's anxiety.

After choosing your conflict, plan how you will establish the tone of your story by answering the following questions:

1. What is my attitude toward the conflict and the characters involved in it?

2. What details can I use to create this mood, or evoke these emotions, in the reader?

Point of View You may tell your story from either the first-person or third-person point of view.

In the first-person point of view, the story is narrated, using the pronoun *I*, by one person who either participates in or witnesses the conflict. Only the narrator's thoughts are expressed, as in the example below.

> *Rapping my knuckles on her desk, I demanded her reply. But she just sat there like a bump.*

In the third-person, or omniscient, point of view, the story is narrated by someone outside the story, someone who knows everything—each character's thoughts and actions. This allows the writer to reveal what any character thinks or does, as in the example below.

Rapping her knuckles on Christie's desk, Mary demanded to know where Christie had hidden the chocolate. But having no intention of giving away her secret, Christie stubbornly ignored the inquiry.

Before you begin writing your imaginative story, you must choose an appropriate point of view from which to tell about the conflict.

Characters To create a captivating story, you must develop interesting and believable characters. Engaged in a struggle, the main character, or *protagonist*, might be opposed by another character, an *antagonist*. There may be other characters as well.

As you develop your characters, attempt to keep them consistent in their behavior and show logical reasons for any change in their behavior. For example, if an ordinarily greedy character suddenly acts generous, you must explain why.

Invent your characters by noting their physical appearance, actions, and personality traits.

Dialogue Dialogue is the spoken words of characters. A character's words can reveal things about the character's personality, background, thoughts, and attitudes. You can use dialogue to develop your characters and make your story more interesting.

Spend a few minutes brainstorming in order to gather ideas about your main characters. Give each one a name, some physical attributes, and a distinctive personality.

Setting The setting is the time and place of the action. Vivid, specific details help to describe the setting of a story. You must consider both location and time. Does your story take place indoors, in a specific room, or outdoors, on a mountain, beach, or prairie? Or does it take place on an airplane, boat, or train? Do the events occur in the morning, afternoon, or evening? Does the story happen in the past, present, or future?

Decide where and when your story will take place and jot down a few details that you can use later to describe your setting.

Plot The plot is the action of your story. Once you have chosen a conflict, one or more characters, and the setting of your story, you are ready to develop the action using this story plan:

BEGINNING OF STORY

Present your characters.

Establish the setting and tone.

Introduce the conflict.

MIDDLE OF STORY

List a series of actions that build to a climax.

END OF STORY

Resolve the conflict, or show why it cannot be resolved.

Use the plan above to make notes, which you can expand later into a full imaginative story.

Practice Follow the instructions in this lesson for brainstorming, choosing a conflict, deciding on the tone and point of view, inventing characters, describing the setting, and planning the plot of your imaginative story. On a separate piece of paper, answer the following questions:

1. Who are your characters? Give a brief description of each.

2. What is the setting? Give the time and place.

3. Describe the tone, the emotions the reader will experience.

4. What is the conflict?

5. Briefly list some actions that will build to a climax.

6. How will you resolve the conflict?

Keep your answers to these questions in your folder or binder. In the next lesson, you will use this information as you write your imaginative story.

LESSON 25

Writing an Imaginative Story

In Lesson 24, you prepared to write your imaginative story. By brainstorming, you gathered ideas and details. You chose a conflict, you decided on the tone and point of view, you invented characters, you described your setting, and you roughly planned the plot. Now you are ready to write the imaginative story.

Keep this plan in front of you as you write:

> BEGINNING OF STORY
>
> Present your characters.
>
> Establish the setting and tone.
>
> Introduce the conflict.
>
> MIDDLE OF STORY
>
> List a series of actions that build to a climax.
>
> END OF STORY
>
> Resolve the conflict, or show why it cannot be resolved.

Practice Using your notes from Lesson 24 and the plan above, follow the steps below to write your story.

1. Write an introductory sentence that will grab the reader's attention.

2. At the beginning of the story, in whatever order you think is best, establish the setting and tone, present your characters, and introduce the conflict.

3. Add dialogue in order to reveal more about your characters' personalities, thoughts, and motivations.

4. Keep the point of view consistent throughout the story.

5. Write a series of actions that build to a climax.

6. Resolve the conflict at the end of your story, or show why it cannot be resolved.

LESSON 26

Evaluating the Imaginative Story

Because *writing is a process* and all of our writing is "work in progress," we constantly make changes to improve our work.

Evaluating Your Writing

In Lesson 25, you completed your imaginative story. Now that some time has passed, you are ready to evaluate it using the following guidelines.

Ask yourself these questions:

- Does my introductory sentence capture the reader's attention?

- Does the beginning of the story establish the tone and suggest the conflict?

- Are the characters believable and interesting?

- Have I revealed the characters' personalities and motivations through dialogue and action as well as description?

- Are my characters consistent in their behavior? Have I adequately explained any changes from their normal behavior?

- Are there other details, modifiers, comparisons, or sensory expressions I could add to help the reader to visualize the setting?

- Do the actions flow logically from one to another?

- Do the actions build suspense?

- Does the dialogue sound natural?

- Does the point of view remain constant throughout the story?

- Are some of my sentences weak or confusing? Should any be removed because they do not relate to the story?

- Do my sentences appear in the best possible order? Could I place them in a different order that is more logical or effective?

- Is each sentence constructed as well as it should be? *Read each sentence in each paragraph as if it were the only sentence on the page. This helps you to catch sentence fragments, run-on sentences, misspellings, and grammatical errors.*

- Is the end of the story believable and satisfying? Has the conflict been resolved?

<u>Practice</u> Use the Evaluation Form on the page following this lesson to evaluate the imaginative story you wrote for Lesson 25. Read your story carefully as you check for the items listed on the Evaluation Form. Write YES or NO in the blank next to each question.

When you are finished, you will either be confident that you have a strong imaginative story, or you will know where it needs to be improved.

If you answered NO to one or more of the questions on the Evaluation Form, rewrite to improve those areas.

When you can answer YES to every question on the Evaluation Form, you will have completed this assignment.

Imaginative Story Evaluation Form

Title: _____

_____ Does my introductory sentence capture the reader's attention?

_____ Does the beginning of the story establish the tone and suggest the conflict?

_____ Are the characters believable and interesting?

_____ Have I revealed the characters' personalities and motivations through dialogue and action as well as description?

_____ Are my characters consistent in their behavior? Have I adequately explained any change from their normal behavior?

_____ Have I included sufficient details, modifiers, comparisons, and sensory expressions to enable the reader to visualize the setting?

_____ Do the actions flow logically from one to another?

_____ Do the actions build suspense?

_____ Does the dialogue sound natural?

_____ Does the point of view remain consistent throughout the story?

_____ Is each sentence strong and clear? Does each sentence relate to the story?

_____ Is each sentence structured as well as it could be? *Read each sentence in each paragraph as if it were the only sentence on the page. This helps you catch fragments and run-on sentences and evaluate the overall strength or weakness of each sentence.*

_____ Is the end of the story believable and satisfying? Has the conflict been resolved?

Writing a Chapter Summary

A summary is a relatively brief restatement of the main ideas in something one has read. In a summary, the writer omits details and condenses a long passage—a whole story, chapter, or book—to its main ideas. Therefore, the summary is much shorter than the original passage.

In this lesson, we shall practice writing a one-paragraph summary of a chapter in a novel.

Chapter Summary If you were reading a novel to a friend and if your friend fell asleep during one of the chapters, he or she might miss a great deal of the action or story line. Your brief *summary* of that missing chapter could help your friend to go on quickly to the next chapter without confusion and without rereading the entire chapter.

Example Below is a summary of *The Phantom Tollbooth*, Chapter 1.

> In this chapter we meet Milo, the main character, who is one day very bored, so he goes to his room. In his room, Milo finds a package, and inside is a tollbooth. The tollbooth comes with tokens to get Milo from place to place. The places are strange places that Milo has never heard of before. Milo decides to go to Dictionopolis, which is very far away. When we finish this chapter, Milo is on his way to Dictionopolis.
>
> Summary by Lilah Arenas

Practice In a single paragraph, summarize one chapter of a novel you are reading or have read in the past (or a novel from the list below). Your paragraph should not exceed eight sentences. Your summary should include major characters and provide a sense of what happens in the chapter.

Suggested novels for this exercise:

The Wizard of Oz by Frank L. Baum

The Secret Garden by Frances Hodgson Burnett

A Tale of Two Cities by Charles Dickens

The Jungle Book by Rudyard Kipling

A Wrinkle in Time by Madeleine L'Engle

The Lion, the Witch, and the Wardrobe by C.S. Lewis

Writing a Short Story Summary

We have learned that a summary condenses a longer passage to a shorter one, leaving out details and giving only the main ideas of the original passage.

In this lesson, we shall practice writing a one-paragraph summary of a short story.

Short Story Summary If you had read an interesting short story and wanted to tell a friend about it, you might give your friend a *summary* of the story. You would not tell the *whole* story or give away the ending. Instead, you would summarize, giving some general information about the main characters, setting, and major conflict.

Example Below is a summary of the short story "Rikki-tikki-tavi" by Rudyard Kipling.

> Rikki-tikki, a baby mongoose, gets washed away in a flood and ends up lying in the hot sun in the middle of a garden path, looking like he's dead. A little boy named Teddy finds Rikki-tikki and tells his parents. Teddy's father rescues the little mongoose, and the family decides to keep him as a pet. An evil cobra named Nag and his equally evil wife, Nagaina, are afraid because mongooses kill snakes, so they try to kill Teddy and his family, hoping that Rikki-tikki will then go away also. Overhearing Nag and Nagaina's plan to kill Teddy and his family, Rikki-tikki makes his own heroic plan to kill the cobras.

Summary by Abby Grace Remington

<u>Practice</u> Write a one-paragraph summary of the imaginative story that you wrote for Lesson 25. Your paragraph should not exceed eight sentences. Your summary should include general information about main characters, setting, and plot.

<u>Additional Practice</u> Read one of the short stories suggested below or one that your teacher suggests. Then put the book away and write a one-paragraph summary of the story. Your paragraph should not exceed eight sentences. Your summary should include general information about main characters, setting, and plot.

Suggested reading:

"The Great Stone Face" by Nathaniel Hawthorne

"Old Times on the Mississippi" by Mark Twain

"Old Yeller" by Fred Gipson

"The Christmas Carol" by Charles Dickens
"The Human Comedy" by William Saroyan
"On Borrowed Time" by Paul Osborn

Preparing to Write Poetry

Writing poetry allows us to tap into our imagination and experience and to use all we have learned about descriptive writing. To write a poem, we must focus our full attention on our subject in order to express impressions, emotions, and images related to it.

As we write poetry, we can communicate our feelings through rhythms and repeated sounds as well as through the words we choose. In this lesson, we shall discuss traditional poetry, free verse, and some simple steps for selecting a subject and gathering thoughts in preparation for writing a poem.

Traditional Poetry

The following poem is an example of **traditional poetry,** the type of poetry established long ago, which has a regular rhythmic, rhyming pattern.

> We search the world for truth; we cull
> The good, the pure, the beautiful,
> From graven stone and written scroll,
> And all old flower-fields of the soul;
> And, weary seekers of the best,
> We come back laden from the quest,
> To find that all the sages said
> Is in the Book our mothers read.
>
> JOHN GREENLEAF WHITTIER (1807–1892)

Free Verse

In contrast to traditional poetry, **free verse** does not have a regular rhyme or rhythm pattern and is frequently used by writers today. The following poem, titled "Silence," is an example of free verse.

> My father used to say,
> "Superior people never make long visits,
> have to be shown Longfellow's grave
> or the glass flowers at Harvard.
> Self-reliant like the cat—
> that takes its prey to privacy,
> the mouse's limp tail hanging like a shoelace
>   from its mouth—
> they sometimes enjoy solitude,

and can be robbed of speech
by speech which has delighted them.
The deepest feeling always shows itself in silence;
not in silence, but restraint."
Nor was he insincere in saying, "Make my
house your inn."
Inns are not residences.

MARIANNE MOORE (1887–1972)

Although the free verse above does not contain rhyme or regular rhythm, it is full of clear, sharp images. Notice the simile, "Self-reliant like the cat…".

Selecting a Subject

In selecting a subject for a poem, make a list of things about which you feel strongly. Using the lines provided, write your ideas for each of the following:

• an important person in your life

_____

• a place you remember with strong emotion

_____

• an activity that you love or hate

_____

•your most or least favorite season or time of day

_____

• your most or least favorite holiday

_____

• a meaningful experience or observation

_____

• a possession that you value

_____

• music that you enjoy or dislike

_____

- your most or least favorite animal

_____

- your most or least favorite food

_____

- an object that you appreciate or despise

_____

After writing one or more ideas under each category above, think about why you feel strongly about each item. Then circle three that you would consider using as the subject of a poem.

Gathering Thoughts about your Subject

Using a separate sheet of paper, brainstorm about at least one of your three possible subjects circled above, as in the following example:

<del>grandma's house</del>

fresh-baked cookies and pies
aroma of coffee
exploring the attic
old toys and bicycles
fun with cousins
hide-and-seek
laughter and singing
the candy dish
tire swing
picking cherries

rose garden
Grandpa playing the saxophone
Uncle Rob on the banjo
a photo album
the cuckoo clock

After brainstorming, place a check mark beside the ideas that most clearly express your feelings. Copy those onto another sheet of paper leaving plenty of space between each one for more details. Then write as many specific details as you can

to fully describe each expression, as in the following
example:

> √ a photo album
>   dust that tickles my nose
>   yellowed with age, fragile pages that crinkle as I turn them
>   black and white photographs of prim and proper ancestors whom
>   I never knew, peculiar-looking people from the old country, such as
>   Great Aunt Lottie with stern expression, thin lips that make a straight
>   line, piercing eyes, tight-fitting dark gown with many buttons
>   and white ruffles at the neck

Practice   Complete the steps given in this lesson for selecting a subject
and gathering thoughts for your own poem. Save your notes
in your folder or binder so that you can add to them at any
time. You will use these notes for writing poems in the next
two lessons.

Writing a Traditional Poem

We have learned that a traditional poem has regular rhythm and rhyme. In this lesson, we shall discuss a few different ways to create rhythm and rhyme in a traditional poem.

Rhythm   Rhythm is the regular repetition or orderly recurrence of sounds or accented syllables. To create rhythm, we combine words to take advantage of their natural accents. Notice the alternating stressed and unstressed syllables in the following lines:

> A gi/ant li/zard held/ my hand
> And star/ted dan/cing with/ the band

ANONYMOUS

> Tell me/ not, in/ mournful/ numbers,
> Life is/ but an/ empty/ dream.

HENRY WADSWORTH LONGFELLOW

While most traditional poetry has a regular rhythmic pattern, this pattern may not be the same in every line. It may change from one line to another, remaining consistent within the whole poem, as in the example below. Notice that the first and third lines each have five accents while the second and fourth lines each have only three accents.

> Brave/ men/ who work/ while o/thers sleep
> Who dare/ while o/thers fly—
> They/ build/ a na/tions pi/llars deep
> And lift/ them to/ the sky.

RALPH WALDO EMERSON

Rhyme   In addition to rhythmic patterns, we can create rhyming patterns to enhance our poetry. Patterns of repeated sounds may be regular or random. They may occur at the beginning, middle, or end of lines. Traditional poetry contains regular rhyme as well as regular rhythm. In Ralph Waldo Emerson's poem above, the last word in every other line of the stanza (a grouping of lines in a poem) rhymes. However, James

Whitcomb Riley's poem below is written in couplets, two successive rhyming lines that form a unit:

Away

I cannot say and I will not say
That he is dead—he is just away!
With a cheery smile and a wave of the hand
He has wandered into an unknown land.
And left us dreaming how very fair
It needs must be since he lingers there
And you—O you, who the wildest yearn
For the old-time step and the glad return,
Think of him faring on, as dear
In the love of There as the love of Here.

Another common rhyming pattern is the limerick, which is often used in humorous poetry and follows an AABBA rhyme scheme, meaning that each limerick is made up of two couplets plus a fifth line that rhymes with the first two, as in the example below:

[A]   There once was a miser named Clarence
[A]   Who Simonized both of his parents;
[B]   "The initial expense,"
[B]   he remarked, "is immense,
[A]   But it saves on the wearance and tearance."

OGDEN NASH

Practice   Using some of the ideas you developed in the previous lesson, write a traditional poem of at least four lines with regular rhyme and rhythm. Try to rhyme important words with words that support the meaning of your poem. Be mindful of stressed and unstressed syllables as you create a rhythm with your words.

Writing a Free-verse Poem

We have learned that free verse does not have regular rhyme or rhythm. In free verse, repeated sounds are more likely to be irregular and inexact, like the sounds of speech. Sensory details and vivid language create clear images and strong messages. In this lesson, we shall use all we have learned about descriptive writing and poetry to create our own free-verse poem.

Repeated Sounds

In free verse, repeated sounds may occur at the beginning, middle, or end of lines. They may be in the form of *assonance*, the repetition of a particular vowel sound; *consonance*, the repetition of a particular consonant sound within or at the end of words; or *alliteration,* the repetition of identical or similar sounds at the beginning of words.

ASSONANCE: nine fine rhymes entwined

CONSONANCE: Pale Dolly, sallow and ill

ALLITERATION: baseball batter with bulging biceps

In addition to the types of repeated sounds above, free verse may employ rhyming words, but they are not confined to a certain pattern as in traditional poetry. For example, a line of free verse might include these words: ache/fake/snake/lake

Figurative Language

In writing free verse, poets also use figurative language, or *figures of speech*, which include the simile, the metaphor, and the personification. We have learned to create vivid descriptions using sensory detail and comparisons such as similes and metaphors. We remember that the simile expresses similarity between two things by using the word *like* or *as*:

The ungodly are...*like* the chaff which the wind drives away. PSALM 1:4, NEW KING JAMES VERSION

All we *like* sheep have gone astray.
ISAIAH 53:6, NEW KING JAMES VERSION

For He shall grow up before Him *as* a tender plant,
And *as* a root out of dry ground.
ISAIAH 53:2, NEW KING JAMES VERSION

The metaphor, on the other hand, describes one thing as though it were another thing:

We are His people and the sheep of His pasture.

PSALM 100:8, NEW KING JAMES VERSION

His truth shall be your shield and buckler.

PSALM 91:4, NEW KING JAMES VERSION

Another form of figurative language is *personification*, a metaphor in which human qualities are given to nonliving things, abstract ideas, or animals. Notice how the moon is personified in the following metaphor:

The moon smiled down on the children and winked…

Simile, metaphor, and personification will enhance your free verse.

Practice Using the ideas you developed in Lesson 29, or some new ideas, write a free-verse poem of at least eight lines. Concentrate on important words that express your ideas, and put them in a meaningful order. Try to create clear, vivid images using sensory details—sights, sounds, smells, and other physical sensations. In addition, you might use simile, metaphor, or personification as well as repeated sounds.

Answers for Practice

Review Lesson

<u>When Misty came home from school, she discovered that her cat, Scamp, was missing</u>. First she walked up and down the street, calling his name. Then she searched through the garage, the backyard, and the front yard. Just as she was ready to give up the search, Misty found Scamp sleeping peacefully behind the sofa in the living room.

During math and social studies, Dudley draws cute little elves in his notebook with a pencil. Sometimes science lectures inspire him to draw exotic plants and animals. His notebook is full of intricate and interesting sketches. <u>Dudley is an outstanding doodler</u>!

<u>I've never seen a bird as peculiar as the heron</u>. A wading bird found in temperate and tropical regions, the heron has long thin legs with knobby knees. Its neck is so long and slender that I wonder how it can swallow anything. Its pointed bill and unusual head feathers give the heron an appearance unlike any other bird I've seen.

Lillian has read hundreds of stories about the wild West, and she can recite them all word for word. <u>Lillian dreams of becoming a cowgirl someday</u>. You'll never see her wearing anything but Western attire—jeans with chaps, boots, and a bandana. Although she doesn't own a horse, she is saving her money to buy one.

Lesson 1

1. The ability to communicate clearly and effectively in writing connects us with people and enhances our prospects for future success in school and in the workplace.

2. Why should we learn to write well?

3. In the first place, writing well allows us to communicate with other people.

4. In the first place…

5. In conclusion…

Lesson 13

I. Grammatical terms
  A. Parts of speech
    1. Noun
    2. Pronoun
    3. Verb
    4. Adverb
    5. Adjective
    6. Preposition
    7. Interjection
    8. Conjunction
  B. Parts of a sentence
    1. Subject
    2. Predicate
    3. Direct object
    4. Indirect object

  C. Punctuation marks
    1. Period
    2. Comma
    3. Semicolon
    4. Colon
    5. Dash
    6. Question mark
    7. Quotation marks
    8. Exclamation mark

(Subtopics may be in any order.)

Circle the simple subject and underline the simple predicate in each sentence. If the subject is understood, write "(you)" after the sentence.

1. Are vegetables nutritious?

2. Please pass the broccoli.

3. Spinach contains iron.

4. My rabbit hates carrots.

5. He prefers alfalfa.

6. Blanca fried some yucca.

7. Will you stay for dinner?

8. Have you eaten your vegetables?

9. James has eaten four servings.

10. Please taste the delicious zucchini.

11. Where are the green beans?

12. Robert has hidden them under a napkin.

13. Do you like sweet potatoes?

14. Isabel baked some in the oven last night.

15. Frozen peas in a bag make a good ice pack for injuries.

16. The chef with the tall white hat went home.

17. Will he return tomorrow?

18. Would you like more squash or mashed potatoes?

19. This summer, I have been growing cucumbers.

20. Here comes dessert!

Circle each letter that should be capitalized in these sentences.

1. asia, the largest continent in the world, is connected by land to europe.

2. therefore, europe and asia together are often called eurasia.

3. the second largest continent is africa.

4. north america and south america are next in size after africa.

5. they are separated from europe, asia, and africa by the atlantic ocean and the pacific ocean.

6. north and south america were once connected by the isthmus of panama, but the panama canal now separates these continents.

7. the frozen continent of antarctica lies at the bottom of the world.

8. the continent of europe is in the eastern hemisphere.

9. china, india, and pakistan are also in the eastern hemisphere.

10. john and james attended pasadena city college in california.

11. mr. rivas studies greek and hebrew at princeton theological seminary.

12. mr. torres has lived in memphis, tennessee; alberta, canada; and quito, ecuador.

13. the amazon river runs through brazil in south america.

14. this june we will hike in the rocky mountains.

15. el salvador, guatemala, honduras, and costa rica are part of central america.

16. did mr. tseng visit havana, cuba last tuesday?

17. have you seen the empire state building in new york city?

18. the london bridge now stands at lake havasu.

19. the months of july and august are hot and dry in the mojave desert.

Underline the entire verb phrase in each sentence.

1. Laura Ingalls was born in 1867 in the country outside Minneapolis.

2. Her parents had grown up on the Wisconsin frontier.

3. Her mother, Caroline, may have been the first white newborn in Brookfield outside Milwaukee.

4. Laura's parents had joined the westward pioneer movement into the vast Dakota prairie.

5. At that time, the U. S. government was giving Dakota farmland to pioneer families.

6. Laura's family must have been the first residents of De Smet, South Dakota.

7. Laura had started her book in the 1920s.

8. *Little House in the Big Woods* was published in 1931.

9. Have you read this novel?

10. It may have been the most popular children's story at that time.

11. Young readers must have been curious.

12. What would happen next?

13. The country has changed since Laura's time.

14. The Big Woods have vanished.

15. The Ingalls clan had remained a poor, homesteading family.

16. Charles Ingalls was known for his scrupulous fairness.

17. He had been hired by the Chicago and Northwestern railroad.

18. Have you visited the Laura Ingalls Wilder Museum?

Slapstick Story #1

Teacher instructions: Have students number blank, lined papers from 1 to 27. Ask them to write an example of the indicated part of speech beside each number. Proceed slowly, and be sure each student has written a correct example of the part of speech you have requested for each blank space in the story.
Next, give students a copy of the story, and ask them to write each word from their list into the blanks with the corresponding numbers.
Finally, ask students to read their stories aloud.

(1)_____ and (2)_____ were
   proper noun (person)   proper noun (person)

planning a trip together. They wanted to see the world, so

they began to write an itinerary. First, they would drive to

(3)_____. From there, they would
   proper noun (place)

(4)_____ or (5)_____ to
   present tense action verb   present tense action verb

(6)_____where they would meet
   proper noun (place)

(7)_____ and (8)_____ and see the
   proper noun (person)   proper noun (person)

famous (9)_____. They would photograph the
          comcrete plural noun

lovely (10)_____ at that location, and then
           concrete singular noun

(11)_____ on the way to (12)_____.
   present tense action verb   proper noun (place)

There, they would visit their (13)_____ and have
                                   feminine noun

lunch with her.

The next day, they would sail to (14)_____ to
                                     proper noun (place)

study (15)_____ and (16)_____ in that
       abstract proper noun   abstract common noun

region. A (17)_____ full of (18)_____
           masculine noun   abstract common noun

and (19)_____ would meet them at the dock to take
     abstract common noun

them to view the splendid (20)_____ and the many
                              concrete singular n.

(21)_____. Finally, they would reach their ultimate
   concrete plural noun

destination, (22)_____.
              proper noun (place)

"This is the perfect itinerary!" they exclaimed to one

another. "We are a (23)_____!" To celebrate, they
                     collective noun

(24)_____ and (25)_____. In exchange
   past tense action verb   past tense action verb

for some (26)_____, their friend,
          common plural noun

(27)_____ offered to make their reservations for
   proper noun (person)

them and buy their tickets online.

More Practice Lesson 20

Circle each letter that should be capitalized in these sentences.

1. we remember sir thomas More for his literary work *utopia,* which describes an imaginary ideal society.

2. abraham lincoln said, "truth is generally the best vindication against slander."

3. have you read the poem "paul revere's ride" by henry wadsworth longfellow?

4. ralph waldo emerson wrote, "it is better to suffer injustice than to do it."

5. geoffrey chaucer's *the canterbury tales* shows the life of fourteenth-century english society.

6. henry ward beecher once said, "it is not work that kills men; it is worry."

7. in *the book of martyrs,* john foxe wrote about martyrs of the christian church.

8. robert leighton said, "god's choice acquaintances are humble [people]."

9. in the late 1500s, edmund spenser wrote his masterpiece, *the faerie queen,* an allegorical, epic romance.

10. curious, benito asked, "why did delilah cut samson's hair?

11. president dwight d. eisenhower said, "the spirit of man is more important than mere physical strength, and the spiritual fiber of a nation than its wealth."

12. a puritan named john trapp once said, "conscience is god's spy and man's overseer."

13. like spenser's *faerie queen,* john bunyan's *pilgrim's progress* is an allegory, a narrative in which the characters and places are symbols.

14. i. electric energy   ii. radiant energy
    a. charge   a. light
    b. circuits   b. colors

15. in the book of *hebrews,* god promises, "i will never leave you, nor forsake you."

Circle each letter that should be capitalized in these sentences.

1. i think aunt sukey puts green beans in her apple pies.

2. have you ever taken professor cuilty's world history class?

3. miss farris teaches english at arroyo high school.

4. do grandma and grandpa petersen speak danish?

5. on sunday, father o'rourke recited the catholic mass in latin.

6. will mom meet aunt christie for breakfast?

7. at the hospital, rabbi cohen comforted the grieving family by reading from the torah.

8. the koran is islam's holy book.

9. i believe dr. bebb is a surgeon at huntington memorial hospital.

10. has lieutenant mussuli retired from the u. s. air force?

11. after a twelve-month tour of duty, captain rice returned from the persian gulf.

12. he had written many letters to his mother in wyoming.

13. the arabic term for god is allah.

14. most muslims believe in repaying evil with good.

15. both christians and muslims believe in a final judgment of god.

16. in april, uncle william will fly from albany, new york to anchorage, alaska.

17. jenan and jumana baked armenian bread for their sister nadia.

18. yesterday, dr. iriye talked to quan about japanese history.

19. i heard that cousin nancy has a russian wolfhound.

20. was president ishigaki in favor of the new statute in our club's by-laws?

Slapstick Story #2

Writing a Book

Follows Lesson 27

After pondering the mysteries of (1)_____ and
abstract proper noun

(2)_____, (3)_____ and
abstract proper noun   _proper noun (person)_

(4)_____ were inspired to write a book. First, they
proper noun (person)

agreed, "We (5)_____ and we (6)_____
1st person future tense action verb   _1st person future tense action verb_

before we begin writing. Also, we shall have

(7)_____ in order to be well prepared for this
present tense infinitive form of verb

task." After (8)_____ and (9)_____ for 20
present participle form of verb   _present participle form of verb_

minutes or so, they had (10)_____ and
past participle form of verb

past participle form of verb (11)_____ long enough to conclude that chapter

one should be titled "How (12)_____." This
present tense infinitive form of verb

chapter would include a section on (13)_____
descriptive adjective

(14)_____ and pictures of a (15)_____
concrete plural noun   _descriptive adjective_

(16)_____ (17)_____ the authors. For
concrete singular noun   _preposition_

clarity, this chapter would discuss (18)_____
abstract common noun

(19)_____ (20)_____ and
preposition   _preposition_

(21)_____ everything.
preposition

Their book would have a (22)_____ cover for
descriptive adjective

eye appeal. The authors felt confident that at least one

person, their friend (23)_____ from
proper noun (person)

(24)_____ would purchase this fine book.
proper noun (place)

Underline each adjective in these sentences.

1. Three main climate zones include the frigid zone, the temperate zone, and the torrid zone.

2. The polar climate of the frigid zone causes a frozen ice cap throughout the entire year.

3. In the tundra climate of this frigid zone, some plants will grow, but no trees will grow.

4. The taiga climate of the temperate zone allows for vast forests of conifer trees.

5. The marine climate has moderate temperatures and much rain and is found on west coasts of some continents.

6. The continental steppe is a treeless plain with cold winters, hot summers, and little rainfall.

7. In the interiors of some continents, we find the humid continental climate with hot summers, cold winters, and much rainfall.

8. The humid subtropic climate has hot, moist summers, mild winters, thick forests, and dense populations.

9. This climate is found on east coasts of continents.

10. The subtropical desert, on the other hand, produces hot, dry summers and cold, dry winters.

11. The Mediterranean climate has a mild, rainy winter and a hot, dry summer.

12. Luscious citrus fruits, olive trees, and cedar trees grow in this type of temperate zone.

13. The tropical rain forest in the torrid zone is known for its scorching heat, humid atmosphere, tall trees, and heavy vines.

14. Many interesting animals live in the savanna where tall, tough grasses and some trees grow.

15. Mr. Haroon's safari took him to remote places.

16. Few people have visited these regions.

17. His jeep lost its brakes as it thundered down a steep, bumpy road.

18. Several swift gnus with curved horns came to the rescue.

Circle each letter that should be capitalized in these sentences.

1. dr. and mrs. ng attend the baptist church on emmons drive.

2. i believe rabbi feingold lives in the northwest.

3. next saturday we will accompany mrs. yu to the arcadia public library.

4. we find books such as *genesis, exodus, leviticus, numbers,* and *deuteronomy* in the old testament part of the bible.

5. catholics, presbyterians, and episcopalians worship jesus christ.

6. mr. yu, a buddhist, came to this country from the far east.

7. we americans are free to worship in our own way.

8. abraham is the forefather of muslims, jews, and christians.

9. where did moses take the hebrew people?

10. anoop reads the koran, the holy book of the islamic faith.

11. when will father o'malley preach again in the southwest?

12. dr. martin luther king, jr. challenged people all over the country, but especially in the south.

13. as world war II was ending, ruth gruber helped thousands of jewish refugees to escape nazi terror and make their homes in our country.

14. wassim, a muslim, worships allah.

15. of course, rabbi golden was reading from the torah.

16. dear freddy,
    please wait for me after school.
                love,
                beth

Circle every capital letter that does not belong in these sentences.

1. In his Physical Education class, Michael played Water Polo and Football.

2. At the Zoo, I saw an African Rhinoceros and a Hippopotamus.

3. In addition to English Walnuts, Colonel Mustard grows Pecans and Washington Apples.

4. His wife has planted Pansies, Marigolds, and African Violets.

5. Would you like French Vanilla or Dutch Chocolate Ice Cream?

6. Until she caught the German measles, Lana was enrolled in Geometry, Biology, and Astronomy.

7. Beth likes Tamales and Enchiladas, but Freddy prefers Chinese Food.

8. Next Spring, we will plant Cucumbers, Green Beans, and Italian Squash.

9. Our Apricots, Peaches, and Plums ripen in early Summer.

10. In the Fall, our Friends, the Lopezes, will move to the South.

11. During the Winter, the Black Squirrels burrow under the snow.

12. I believe Mr. Zee is recovering from a bad case of Conjunctivitis that he caught from his Gnu.

13. Last Summer, he suffered from Gastroenteritis after eating too much New York Cheese Cake.

14. He has been playing Hide-And-Seek and Ping Pong for entertainment.

15. My Mom made Swiss Cheese sandwiches for lunch and Chocolate Eclairs for dessert.

16. Elspeth found a Japanese Beetle in her Chicken Casserole.

Diagram each sentence in the space to the right.

1. Marie Curie, Albert Einstein, and Galileo Galilei made amazing discoveries.

2. Florence Nightengale encouraged and trained other nurses.

3. She reformed hospitals and nursing schools.

4. She gave hospitals and nurses new ideas.

5. Florence Nightengale, tireless and determined, improved the nursing profession.

6. Marie and Pierre discovered radium and polonium.

Place commas wherever they are needed in these sentences.

1. On June 28 1914 a Serbian assassinated the heir to the Austrian throne.

2. World War I began on July 28 1914 when Austria declared war on Serbia.

3. Russia mobilized for conflict on July 30 1914.

4. On August 1 1914 Germany declared war on Russia.

5. Then on August 3 Germany declared war on France.

6. The Triple Alliance consisted of Germany Austria-Hungary and Italy.

7. The Triple Entente included Great Britain France and Russia.

8. On April 6 1917 Congress declared war on Germany.

9. Private organizations like the Red Cross the YMCA the Salvation Army the Knights of Columbus and the Jewish Welfare Board helped in the war effort.

10. On November 11 1918 in Compiègne France representatives of the Allies and of Germany signed an armistice to end the war.

11. The Peace Conference convened January 18 1919 at Versailles outside of Paris France.

12. President Woodrow Wilson collapsed after delivering a speech in Pueblo Colorado on September 25 1919.

13. The White House is located at 1600 Pennsylvania Avenue Washington D.C.

For 14–16, place commas where they are needed in these addresses.

14. 11147 Bunbury Street Saint Louis Missouri

15. 270 Alta Vista Drive Tallahassee Florida

16. 4921 Cedar Avenue Topeka Kansas

17. 30 Pine Street Denver Colorado

Slapstick Story #3

Starting a Business

Follows Lesson 45

To earn money for college, (1)_____ and (proper noun (person))

(2)_____ decided to become partners in a business (proper noun (person))

venture. After (3)_____ and (4)_____, (present participle form of verb) (present participle form of verb)

(5)_____, (6)_____, and (preposition) (preposition)

(7)_____ the library, they found (preposition)

(8)_____ (9)_____ books to help them (number adjective) (descriptive adjective)

research possibilities for a new business. Some of the books

comparative adjective were (10)_____ than others. The

(11)_____ was a book written by their friend (superlative adjective)

(12)_____ from (13)_____. (proper noun (person)) (proper noun (place))

As they read, new (14)_____ ideas came to (descriptive adjective)

them. They could (15)_____ (16)_____ (present tense transitive verb) (concrete plural noun)

and sell them, or they could (17)_____ (present tense trnasitive verb)

(18)_____ and rent them. Perhaps they could (concrete plural noun)

manufacture (19)_____ or make a movie about (concrete plural noun)

(20)_____ starring (21)_____. (abstract common noun) (proper noun (person))

Adrenaline flowing, they (22)_____ (past tense action verb intransitive)

(23)_____ (24)_____ with excietment. (coordinating conjunction) (past tense action verb intransitive)

The possibilities were endless. Undoubtedly, they would

each earn at least (25)_____ dollars. (number adjective)

Place commas where they are needed in these sentences.

1. Cynthia please write to me!

2. Father Timothy rector of an Episcopal church helps troubled teenagers.

3. Barnabas his huge black dog heeds scripture.

4. Are you wearing clean socks Dooley?

5. I hope Maggie that you will leave your iguana at home.

6. Barbra Farris R.N. worked at a medical clinic in Haiti.

7. Has Dolores Dolorfino M.D. prescribed antibiotics for your infection?

8. May I wash your car for you Mr. Rivas?

9. Richard M. Curtis D.D.S. repaired my broken tooth.

10. I believe Miss Cheung Vice President will conduct the next P.T.A. meeting.

11. Gerry Wilson pastor of the Arcadia Friends Church led the prayer meeting.

12. Hard-working Pac Couch District Attorney won her case in the Supreme Court this morning.

13. Is Mauricio Zelaya Ph.D. the author of that fine editorial?

14. Judy's restaurant sells pepperoni pizza my favorite food.

15. The school principal Mr. Stuart Dunn gave the students a pep talk.

16. I wish dear friend that you lived closer.

17. Anoop Habib a theologian studies the Dead Sea Scrolls.

18. The young school board candidate Andre Quintero posted hundreds of campaign signs.

19. Mom can you hear me?

20. I'm happy Henri that you came to this country.

Place commas where they are needed.

1. Dear Justin
   Please dump the trash.
               Love
               Trevor

2. Hi Trevor
   I dumped the trash.
               Love
               Justin

3. Hey Jared
   I hope you win your soccer game this Saturday.
               Your cousin
               Mariah

4. The index listed "Revere Paul" on page 227.

5. He wrote "Hake Kyle" because it asked for last name first.

6. Sir Isaac Newton an English mathematician and physicist brought the scientific revolution of the seventeenth century to its climax.

7. In fact he established the principal outlines of our system of natural science.

8. In mathematics he was the first person to develop the calculus.

9. The calculus a new and powerful instrument carried modern mathematics above the level of Greek geometry.

10. Newton's three laws of motion I believe became the foundation of modern dynamics.

11. From these three laws of motion he derived the law of universal gravitation.

12. In addition Newton studied optics and the phenomena of colors.

13. To explain how colors arise he proved that sunlight is a mixture of different rays that create different colors.

14. Edmund Halley I understand visited Isaac Newton in 1684.

15. Among other things Halley and Newton discussed orbital motion.

16. After this discussion Newton published his ideas about universal gravitation.

More Practice Lesson 57

Underline the dependent clause in each sentence, and circle the subordinating conjunction.

1. After a Viking tribe, the Russes, invaded, the land became known as the Land of the Rus, or Russia.

2. I have heard that the city of Kiev became the political and religious center of Russia.

3. While the Mongols ruled Russia, the religious center moved from Kiev to Moscow.

4. Ivan III became the first true national leader of Russia after the Mongolian troops were defeated.

5. Because he enslaved workers, Ivan IV became known as Ivan the Terrible.

6. You may remember that other famous czars included Peter the Great, Catherine the Great, and Alexander.

7. Even though Russia was already a huge territory, the czars wanted to expand the empire.

8. While Nicholas I was czar, Russia added many countries to its empire.

9. Since the secret police controlled the press and universities, the government controlled every part of Russian thought and life.

10. Nicholas I crushed a revolt of the Russian people so that the central government kept growing stronger.

11. Although the French emperor Napoleon marched into Moscow, the cold Russian winter defeated his army.

12. When Russian factory workers revolted in 1905, Nicholas II crushed them.

13. As World War I ended, conditions were even worse for the Russian people.

14. While events were building to a breaking point in Russia, the idea of Marxism arose.

15. The working class could control the government as soon as the upper and middle classes were abolished.

16. The government would own all property so that everyone would be "equal."

17. If Marxists wanted a successful Communist government, they would have to kill entire classes of people.

18. After the Bolsheviks overthrew the Russian people's government, Lenin became the leader of the first Communist state in history.

For 1–6, underline each participal phrase and circle the word it modifies.

1. The sailor, weathered by experience, held the rudder.

2. Having given his opinion, Oscar sat down.

3. The man driving that truck is my neighbor.

4. Running around the park, Steve saw an old friend.

5. Having studied for hours, Elmo felt confident about his geometry test.

6. The little boy blowing bubbles is my nephew.

For 7–10, complete the diagram of each sentence.

7. His limping deceived us.

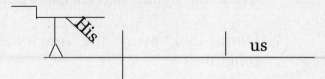

8. Emelina enjoys feeding her pigeons.

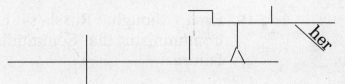

9. Riding a unicycle, Cisco impressed the crowd.

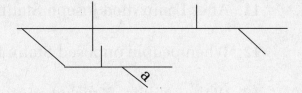

10. Having finished the race, we rested.

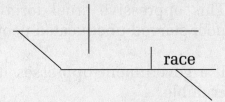

Place commas where they are needed in these sentences.

1. Although the Russian people resisted Lenin's Communism Lenin forced his power upon them.

2. Since Communists ruled the government took control of all land and major industries.

3. Food and goods were meagerly distributed by this cruel tyrannical government.

4. As the government took control all private trade was stopped.

5. Because the government owned all property churches were closed or controlled by the government.

6. Though White Russians opposed Communism they were overcome by the Red Russian Communists.

7. Lenin took away the freedoms of speech press and religion.

8. Since human life had no value many "enemies of the state" were executed.

9. Even though Russia's economy collapsed under Communism the Communists would not admit their failure.

10. Artists writers and musicians were forced to work for the government.

11. After Lenin died Joseph Stalin became Russia's dictator.

12. When people opposed Stalin they were killed.

13. While Nikita Krushchev ruled Russia Many Eastern European Nations were taken over by Communists.

14. This oppressive cruel form of government resulted in poor starved uneducated people.

15. If a government oppresses its people it will eventually crumble.

Place commas where they are needed in these sentences.

1. Benjamin Franklin said "Content makes poor men rich; discontent makes rich men poor."

2. In *Othello*, William Shakespeare wrote "Poor and content is rich and rich enough."

3. "The noblest mind the best contentment has" wrote Edmund Spencer in *The Faerie Queen*.

4. "To know what is right and not do it is the worst cowardice" said Confucius.

5. An old French proverb says "Justifying a fault doubles it."

6. Woodrow Wilson said "I believe in democracy because it releases the energies of every human being."

7. On December 14, 1799, George Washington spoke his last words "Doctor, I die hard, but I am not afraid to go."

8. On his deathbed in 1848, John Quincy Adams said "This is the last of earth! I am content."

9. We can have fear or we can have faith.

10. He would not forgive nor would he forget.

11. Unforgiveness embitters the soul but forgiveness brings life.

12. She asked for forgiveness for she was sorry.

13. Envy rots the bones but love heals all wounds.

14. Ben Franklin wrote wise words so we remember them.

15. "Envy is an enemy of honor" says an old proverb.

16. I believe her testimony for she has integrity.

17. The fireman was exhausted yet he continued searching.

18. Referring to the American flag, Charles Sumner said "White is for purity, red for valor, blue for justice."

Place quotation marks where they are needed in these sentences.

1. Oliver Wendell Holmes said, Fame usually comes to those who are thinking about something else.

2. They are able because they think they are able, said Virgil in the *Aeneid*.

3. A Hindu proverb warns, Even nectar is poison if taken in excess.

4. It is better to be the enemy of a wise man, said the Hindu sage, than the friend of a fool.

5. A wise man will make haste to forgive, said Samuel Johnson, because he knows the true value of time, and will not suffer it to pass away in unnecessary pain.

6. A Danish proverb says, There is no need to hang a bell on a fool.

7. Dig a well before you are thirsty, advised the Chinese scholar.

8. Life has taught me to forgive, said Otto Von Bismarck, but to seek forgiveness still more.

9. Free countries are those in which the rights of man are respected, said Robespierre, and the laws, in consequence, are just.

10. Those who deny freedom to others deserve it not for themselves, said Lincoln, and, under a just God, cannot long retain it.

11. Rudyard Kipling said, All we have of freedom—all we use or know—This our fathers bought for us, long and long ago.

12. Freedom exists, said Woodrow Wilson, only where people take care of the government.

13. Leonardo da Vinci advised, Reprove a friend in secret, but praise him before others.

14. A friend should bear his friend's infirmities, wrote Shakespeare.

For 1–16, place quotation marks where they are needed in the dialogs.

We read this dialogue in *The Wizard of Oz* by L. Frank Baum:

1. Where is the Emerald City? he inquired. And who is Oz?

2. Why, don't you know? she returned in surprise.

3. No, indeed; I don't know anything. You see, I am stuffed, so I have no brains at all, he answered sadly.

4. Oh, said Dorothy, I'm awfully sorry for you.

We find this dialogue in *Dr. Jekyll and Mr. Hyde* by Robert Louis Stevenson:

5. Have you the envelope? he asked.

6. I burned it, replied Jekyll, before I thought what I was about. But it bore no postmark. The note was handed in.

7. Shall I keep this and sleep upon it? asked Uterson.

8. I wish you to judge for me entirely, was the reply. I have lost confidence in myself.

We read the following dialog in *Johnny Tremain* by Esther Forbes:

9. Cilla said, You watch him much?

10. He answered a little miserably, It's just like I can't help it. I don't mean ever to think of him.

11. Isannah murmured, What do they do with their pearls?

12. They drink their pearls.

This dialog comes from C.S. Lewis's *The Silver Chair*:

13. Good-bye, dear Puddleglum, said Jill going over to the Marsh-wiggle's bed. I'm sorry we called you a wet blanket.

14. So'm I, said Eustace. You've been the best friend in the world.

15. And I do hope we'll meet again, added Jill.

16. Not much chance of that, I should say, replied Puddleglum. I don't reckon I'm very likely to see my old wigwam either.... *(cont. next page)

For 17–29, enclose titles of short literary works in quotation marks.

17. Oliver Wendell Holmes's poem, Old Ironsides, talks about a warship used in the War of 1812.

18. In his sermon entitled Selfishness, Charles Finney discusses this disease and gives a cure for it.

19. The class laughed heartily at Artemus Ward's two humorous essays, My Life Story and A Business Letter.

20. In Nathaniel Hawthorne's short story, The Great Carbuncle, eight people with varying motives all seek the precious jewel, but it is a risky business.

21. In the computer magazine, Robert read an interesting article, How to Create Your Own Website.

22. Today, the *Mud Valley News* published an editorial titled Educational Experimentation using Guinea Pigs.

23. Edgar Allen Poe's poem titled Alone describes how the author differs from other people.

24. Mr. Hake, a mathematician, gave a lecture entitled The Pythagorean Theorem for Dummies.

25. Washington Irving's article, A Republic of Prairie Dogs, attributes human qualities and characteristics to these little animals.

26. For his science class, Andrew wrote an essay called The Undefinable Black Hole.

27. Benito's short story, Life on the Princeton Levee, gained notoriety on the East Coast.

28. William Shakespeare wrote many longer plays, but he also wrote some short poems such as Under the Greenwood Tree.

29. Francis Bacon (1561–1626), an English philosopher, scientist, and writer, wrote an essay called On Revenge.

More Practice Lesson 72

Underline all words that should be italicized in print.

1. Shall we watch the movie Gone with the Wind, or would you rather see Mary Poppins?

2. "The Dance of the Sugar Plum Fairies" is a song from The Nutcracker.

3. The Zamora Family enjoyed the Phantom of the Opera.

4. Kurt plays and replays his CD entitled Veggie Tunes II.

5. Have you read that enchanting novel, The Hobbit, by J.R.R. Tolkien?

6. The aircraft carrier Enterprise entered the Persian Gulf.

7. We cruised Glacier Bay in Alaska on a ship called The Scandinavian Princess.

8. They saw Mona Lisa, Leonardo da Vinci's famous painting, when they visited the Louvre in Paris.

9. Leonardo da Vinci also painted Lady with an Ermine, which can be seen at the Czartoryski Museum in Cracow, Poland.

10. Years ago, we rode the train, Super Chief, from Los Angeles to Chicago.

11. The university owns a reproduction of Rodin's famous statue, The Thinker.

12. The Statue of Liberty welcomes immigrants to a land of opportunity.

13. In Melville's novel, Moby Dick, the evil Captain Ahab believes that he alone can conquer the white whale.

14. Aunt Isabel reads the Los Angeles Times newspaper every morning.

15. Uncle Gerardo subscribes to a magazine called Country Living.

Complete this irregular verb chart by writing the past and past participle forms of each verb.

	VERB	PAST	PAST PARTICIPLE
1.	beat		
2.	bite		
3.	bring		
4.	build		
5.	burst		
6.	buy		
7.	catch		
8.	come		
9.	cost		
10.	dive		
11.	drag		
12.	draw		
13.	drown		
14.	drive		
15.	eat		
16.	fall		
17.	feel		
18.	fight		
19.	flee		
20.	flow		
21.	fly		
22.	forsake		

Write the correct verb form for each sentence.

1. Yesterday, Arroyo (beated, beat) Rosemead in cross country.

2. Arroyo has (beat, beaten) Rosemead in every meet this season.

3. Hoover (brang, brought) taquitos to share with his friends.

4. In the past, he has (brung, brought) enough for ten.

5. In the 1950s, the L.E. Dixon Company (builded, built) dams in California and Washington.

6. They have also (builded, built) bridges and tunnels.

7. Sam (buyed, bought) me lunch.

8. He has (buyed, bought) me lunch frequently.

9. Hector (catched, caught) the high, fly ball to center field.

10. By the seventh inning, he had (catched, caught) six fly balls.

11. Martha (comed, came) home at noon.

12. She said she had (came, come) to eat lunch.

13. Last Tuesday, apples (costed, cost) 99¢ a pound.

14. They have (cost, costed) less in the past.

15. Kyla (dove, dived) into the pool to rescue her cat.

16. She has (dove, dived) after that cat twice today.

17. Molly and Andrew (drawed, drew) chalk pictures this morning.

18. They have (drew, drawn) several today.

19. Lorna (drived, drove) through the streets in search of Dijon.

20. Dijon has nearly (drove, driven) Lorna crazy.

21. Humpty Dumpty (falled, fell) off the wall this afternoon.

22. Has he ever (falled, fell, fallen) before?

23. The crows and parrots (fighted, fought) over their territory.

24. They have (fighted, fought) every spring.

25. The jet (flied, flew) above the clouds.

26. Christie had never (flew, flown) so high before.

Complete this irregular verb chart by writing the past and past participle forms of each verb.

VERB	PAST	PAST PARTICIPLE
1. give	_____	_____
2. go	_____	_____
3. hang (execute)	_____	_____
4. hang (dangle)	_____	_____
5. hide	_____	_____
6. hold	_____	_____
7. lay	_____	_____
8. lead	_____	_____
9. lend	_____	_____
10. lie (recline)	_____	_____
11. lie (deceive)	_____	_____
12. lose	_____	_____
13. make	_____	_____
14. mistake	_____	_____
15. put	_____	_____
16. raise	_____	_____
17. ride	_____	_____
18. rise	_____	_____
19. run	_____	_____
20. see	_____	_____
21. sell	_____	_____

Underline the correct verb form for each sentence.

1. Silvia and Helen (given, gave) their time to help younger students.

2. They have (gived, gave, given) many hours this week.

3. Rafa and Marta (gone, went) back to Costa Rica yesterday.

4. Have they (gone, went) already?

5. We (hanged, hung) our clothes in the closet.

6. We have (hanged, hung) them all in the closet.

7. Ernie (hided, hid) behind the sofa.

8. He has (hid, hidden) there before.

9. Kerry (holded, held) the sleeping baby.

10. She has (holded, held) the baby all day.

11. Fatima (layed, laid) the catalog on her desk.

12. She has (layed, laid, lain) it there before.

13. Zack felt exhausted, so he (laid, lay) down for a while.

14. He has (laid, lain) there since noon.

15. Unfortunately, I (losed, lost) my library card.

16. Have you (losed, lost) yours also?

17. Emelina (maked, made) pupusas.

18. I thought she had (maked, made) pancakes.

19. One day, she absentmindedly (put, putted) her iron in the refrigerator.

20. Never before had she (put, putted) it there.

21. They (rised, rose) from their seats when the national anthem began.

22. We have always (rose, risen) to salute the flag.

23. They (saw, seen) each other today.

24. They have (saw, seen) each other every day.

25. I believe they have (selled, sold) their home.

Complete this irregular verb chart by writing the past and past participle forms of each verb.

	VERB	PAST	PAST PARTICIPLE
1.	set	_____	_____
2.	shake	_____	_____
3.	shine (light)	_____	_____
4.	shine (polish)	_____	_____
5.	shut	_____	_____
6.	sit	_____	_____
7.	slay	_____	_____
8.	sleep	_____	_____
9.	spring	_____	_____
10.	stand	_____	_____
11.	strive	_____	_____
12.	swim	_____	_____
13.	swing	_____	_____
14.	take	_____	_____
15.	teach	_____	_____
16.	tell	_____	_____
17.	think	_____	_____
18.	wake	_____	_____
19.	weave	_____	_____
20.	wring	_____	_____
21.	write	_____	_____

Underline the correct verb form for each sentence.

1. Last night, I (setted, set) an alarm for 6 a.m.

2. The night before, I had (setted, set) it for 7 a.m.

3. David (shook, shaked) hands with each guest.

4. He has (shook, shaked, shaken) many hands today.

5. The star (shined, shone) brightly in the night sky.

6. It had (shined, shone) brighter the night before.

7. Mr. Peabody (shined, shone) the silverware before the banquet.

8. He has (shined, shone) that silverware faithfully every month.

9. The Cozaks (shutted, shut) their windows because it was windy.

10. Have they (shutted, shut) the windows to keep out the noise?

11. Myrtle the Turtle (sitten, sat) in the sun.

12. She had (sitted, sat) there for hours before I noticed her.

13. Fong (slept, sleeped) through the tornado.

14. Have you ever (slept, sleeped) through a tornado?

15. The grandfather clock (standed, stood) in a corner.

16. It had (standed, stood) there for a hundred years.

17. The little fish (swam, swum) away from the big fish.

18. Has the little fish ever (swam, swum) alongside a big fish?

19. Has Freddy (took, taken) Turbo and Sophie to the dog groomer?

20. Yes, Freddy (took, taken) them to the groomer yesterday.

21. Blanca (teached, taught) me to make albondigas.

22. She has (teached, taught) me to make several delicious dishes.

23. Has Ilbea (telled, told) you her plans?

24. Yes, she (telled, told) me yesterday.

25. Have you (thinked, thought) about learning a foreign language?

26. Yes, I (thinked, thought) I would study Arabic next year.

The Talent Show

Follows Lesson 76

descriptive adjective

The annual spring talent show was just around the corner. The citizens of (1)_____ could hardly wait.
proper noun (place)

(2)_____, (3)_____, and
proper noun (person)   proper noun (person)

(4)_____ formed a (5)_____ in order to
proper noun (person)   collective common noun

work together in anticipation of winning first prize for their

(6)_____ performance. "Our act will be the

(7)_____," they said. "If will be (8)_____
superlative adjective   comparative adjective

than (9)_____. But what shall we do?" they asked
possessive pronoun

each other.

All three were adept at (10)_____ and
present participle form
of verb

(11)_____. They wanted (12)_____ or
present participle form   infinitive form of verb
of verb   present tense

perhaps (13)_____ in order to show off their talent,
infinitive form of verb
present tense

but they were not sure they could beat (14)_____,
proper noun (person)

who would probably do a similar act. They held a meeting

and pondered, (15)_____ and (16)_____
past tense transitive   past tense transitive
verb   verb

subjects such as (17)_____ and
abstract common noun

(18)_____ before they finally came to the
abstract proper noun

conclusion they would sing (19)_____ song(s), one
number adjective

about live and (20)_____, another about sunsets
concrete plural noun

and (21)_____, and another about
abstract common noun

(22)_____ in (23)_____. With this
present participle form   proper noun (place)
of verb

(24)_____ selection of songs, they would surely
descriptive adjective

win first prize. Sadly, however, they dropped out of

competition when they heard rumors that Elvis had entered

the contest.

Underline each adverb in these sentences.

1. Now, I clearly remember what happened yesterday.

2. It was snowing very hard, so I went out to shovel the driveway.

3. I had not quite finished when the snowplow drove by.

4. Rather rudely, the driver laughed and told me I would be shoveling forever.

5. Completely annoyed, I shoveled more energetically to prove to the driver that I was not a weakling.

6. I tossed snow everywhere and barely felt the cold.

7. My family sat cozily inside; they were quite oblivious to my labor.

8. Soon, I looked around and realized that snow still covered the driveway.

9. Then snow began falling too heavily for me to make any progress.

10. I wouldn't give up.

11. Highly motivated to maintain my pride, I shoveled frantically.

12. My neighbor shook her head slightly in disbelief.

13. "It is not very smart to shovel snow today," she said simply.

14. Even more determined, I ignored her.

15. I looked down and never glanced up, so I didn't notice the branch that sagged above.

16. It was heavily loaded with snow.

17. It cracked loudly, but the snow fell silently.

18. I was underneath.

Replace commas with semicolons where they are needed in these sentences.

1. Cities with Native American names include Wichita, Kansas, Tucson, Arizona, Tallahassee, Florida, Minneapolis, Minnesota, and Seminole, Oklahoma.

2. The sales representative passes through Denver, Colorado, Austin, Texas, and Memphis, Tennessee.

3. Damien plays drums, Annie plays the saxophone, the flute, and the trumpet.

4. Okra and artichokes are vegetables, tangarines, apricots, and nectarines are fruits.

5. Dr. Hagelganz spoke this week, moreover, Foster Shannon will speak next week.

6. James washed the car, cleaned the house, and mowed the lawn, consequently, he fell asleep during the movie.

7. I like to bake cookies, cakes, and pies, however, I've never made an eclair.

8. In November a pound of bananas cost 29¢, in December, 39¢, in January, 49¢, in February, 59¢, and in March, 69¢.

9. I worked all day, therefore, I finished the project on time.

10. Donald and Tim will be there, also, Cecilia will come if she can.

11. She enjoys planting trees, for example, she planted two oaks and a cedar last fall.

12. Joe cleaned the kitchen, furthermore, he organized all the cupboards and drawers.

13. The weather was cold, nevertheless, Bob hiked to the top of the mountain.

14. He wore his new shoes, as a result, he has blisters on his feet.

15. Would you rather visit Paris, France, Rome, Italy, Juneau, Alaska, or Moscow, Russia?

Slapstick Story #5

The Invention Convention

Follows Lesson 93

(1)_____ liked (2)_____,
proper noun (person)   _infinitive—present tense_

(3)_____, and (4)_____. He also liked to
infinitive—present tense   _infinitive—present tense_

invent things. At the up-coming invention convention, he

would display (5)_____ (6)_____ new
number adjective   _descriptive adjective_

gismos for which he had obtained patents.

(7)_____, he would begin packing these objects
adverb that tells "when"

(8)_____ for his trip to the convention in
adverb that tells "how"

(9)_____. He searched (10)_____ and
proper noun (place)   _adverb that tells "where"_

(11)_____ for the right-sized boxes and cartons to
adverb that tells "where"

pack his (12)_____, ingenious (13)_____
descriptive adjective   _common, concrete, singular noun_

scraper and his handy, (14)_____
descriptive adjective

(15)_____ shampooer made from recycled
common, concrete, singular noun

(16)_____. Proud of his gadgets, he thought his
common, concrete, plural noun

(17)_____ and (18)_____ device was the
present participle form of verb   _present participle form of verb_

(19)_____ in the world. Indeed, it was
superlative adjective

(20)_____ than any invention of his friend
comparative adjective

(21)_____.
proper noun (person)

However, his favorite, most-prized product was his

(22)_____, new (23)_____ zapper, which
descriptive adjective   _concrete, common noun_

he (24)_____ stowed away in his
adverb that tells "how"

descriptive adjective (25)_____ briefcase to protect it. He thought how

fortunate that his friend, (26)_____ worked for the
proper noun (person)

government patent office.

Insert apostrophes where they are needed in these sentences.

1. She couldnt recall what shed done during the summers of 68 and 70.

2. I cant remember their address, but Im sure it has several 7s.

3. Theyre playing tic-tac-toe; theyre carefully placing their xs and os.

4. "Ive been standin here waitin for twenty minutes," he complained.

5. "Im sorry," she said, "but I didnt see you."

6. Arent malapropisms funny?

7. Wasnt he born in 48?

8. Thats not the only novel weve studied.

9. I think hes a troublemaker, a proponent of dissention.

10. Wouldnt you agree?

11. Perhaps shell counsel him confidentially.

12. If its Monday, youd be smart to elude him entirely.

13. They couldnt see their psychosis from our perspective.

14. Theyve completed the prototype, and theyre ready to try it.

15. Weve heard the parable, but we havent understood its meaning.

16. Shes kept her old customs, but she isnt wearing the traditional costume.

17. If youve synchronized your watches, then youre set to begin.

18. "Whats that screamin noise?" asked Authur.

19. "Bills practicin the saxophone," Max replied.

20. I dont think its treason, but Im sure its a crime.

For 1–4, complete each sentence diagram.

1. Ancient Greeks admired physical fitness; citizens exercised at the public gymnasium.

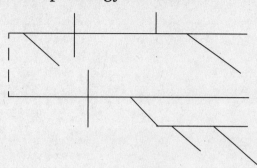

2. Asclepius, who usually carried a snake coiled around his staff, was the Greek god of healing.

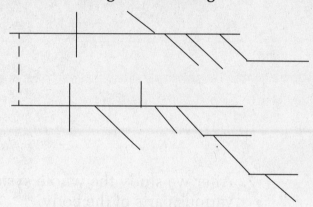

3. Hippocrates carefully observed patients' symptoms before he made a diagnosis.

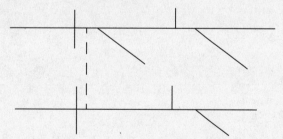

4. Having sworn the Hippocratic oath, Dr. Ngo gave his patients his best effort.

For 5–8, diagram each sentence in the space provided.

5. Developing more successful methods of healing was Hippocrates' goal.

6. Hippocrates, the founder of scientific medicine, practiced and taught on the island of Cos.

7. After we study the whole system, we can understand the various parts of the body.

8. The great Pericles died in a plague since the ancient world had no protection against epidemic diseases.